*For my mom Claire, who travels with me from place
to place to babysit my dogs while I performed my
investigations … and my late father John whose spirit
guides me from heaven, every step of the way.*

© Gerard Lauzon/North Light

About the Author

Andrea Mesich (Ironwood, MI) was a skeptic about the paranormal until she had a dramatic encounter with a ghost in 2004. Since then, she has studied the paranormal, practicing new techniques, testing different theories, and researching history, trying to discover why paranormal events happen and what we can learn from them.

the
ghost
in the
coal
cellar

andrea mesich

true case files from a lone investigator

Llewellyn Publications
Woodbury, Minnesota

FIRST EDITION
First Printing, 2014

Book design by Bob Gaul
Cover design by Kevin R. Brown
Cover image: iStockphoto.com/17919513/©zagorskid
Editing by Ed Day
Interior Photos by Andrea Mesich

Llewellyn Publications is a registered trademark of Llewellyn Worldwide Ltd.

Library of Congress Cataloging-in-Publication Data
Mesich, Andrea.
  The ghost in the coal cellar: true case files from a lone investigator/Andrea Mesich.—First Edition.
     pages cm
  ISBN 978-0-7387-4052-2
  1. Ghosts—United States. 2. Haunted places—United States. 3. Parapsychology.
  I. Title.
  BF1472.U6M47 2014
  133.10973—dc23
                            2014006086

Llewellyn Publications
A Division of Llewellyn Worldwide Ltd.
2143 Wooddale Drive
Woodbury, MN 55125-2989
www.llewellyn.com

Printed in the United States of America

Contents

Introduction

My name is Andrea and I am a paranormal investigator. I have been investigating the paranormal since 2004 when I had my first experience. I had a true level of skepticism about the whole industry. I didn't really believe in ghosts or UFOs, so imagine my fear, my shock, and my wonder when I had a paranormal experience. I was glad my mother was there, mostly because then I knew I wasn't going crazy; she was experiencing the exact same things I was. It wasn't just me.

My first encounter with the paranormal changed my mind completely and, as fear turned to curiosity, I found myself wanting to know more. How did this event come to happen to me? Where did this spirit come from? The haunting, which started in 2004 and continued for several years, was happening in my childhood home. By that point I had lived in that house for nearly thirty years and had never had a paranormal encounter before. After speaking with two well-known investigators, I firmly believe my brother brought a spirit home with him from one of his trips (which always included paranormal investigations of haunted areas).

I have been studying the paranormal ever since. I call myself the paranormal *ronin*. A ronin is the Japanese word for "masterless samurai"; however, instead of a masterless samurai, I am a groupless investigator. I accept the kindness of various groups and join them when invited on investigations. I learn their investigation styles and techniques, then try them out and see what works for me. Over the years, I have learned the best style of investigation is an open ear, a sharp eye, and a good recorder. The rest are bells and whistles, but helpful to investigations in their own way. Most teams are extremely welcoming and willing to share what they know to help me find answers and help me learn what works best for me as an investigator. I also have the opportunity to investigate places I would otherwise not be able to investigate by joining groups from all over. I want to know more about my own experiences and learn how to better help others with their experiences.

I have been many places and experienced many things. It was time I shared my experiences with everyone. That is where this book comes in, dear readers. Through this book,

I will take you through a few of the most haunted places I have ever been to in my time as a paranormal investigator. These are not fictional stories meant to entertain or scare you during a dark and stormy night; these are not tales of high school haunted houses filled with teenagers in costumes that jump out and shout "BOO" as you walk by.

The tales I'm about to walk you through are all real. These are actual accounts of the true paranormal events. You will read eyewitness accounts of the ghostly tales, and follow me on an actual paranormal investigation and see these tales come to life before your very eyes. If you are brave of heart, follow me, friends, into the darkness of the unknown to do what many have done before us; to search to understand what is currently beyond our understanding, and perhaps learn a little bit more about ourselves.

one

The Beginning

. . . .

A study from a few years ago showed that three of every four Americans believed in the paranormal, many believing they have experienced paranormal events. I was not one of those people. I loved ghost stories. Even as a little girl I liked to hear stories like the one about a teenager who picked up a girl on the side of the road looking for a ride home. She left her jacket in his car after he dropped her off and when he returned it to the house he went to the night before, the mother informed him her daughter died in an accident years earlier.

Ghost stories were always exciting, thrilling, and chilling, but to me, ghosts were as real as a Stargate where you could be on earth, walk through the force field, and instantaneously be on an alien planet when you come out the other side. It made for a great movie and then television show, but it wasn't based on reality. The same went for ghost stories and the haunted movies that are always "based on actual events." They always say "based on actual events" because you can't prove it didn't happen...and it makes the story more exciting, like *The Amityville Horror*. At least, that is what I thought back then.

I never gave the paranormal much thought except on dark and stormy nights when I'd curl up in bed with books like *The Canterville Ghost*. All harmless fun. Other than that, I was a typical girl growing up. I had my mom and dad, my two older brothers JP and AP. I never understood why my mom didn't give me a middle name that started with P. I had my inner circle of friends and my beloved pets. I was a good Catholic girl who attended church every Sunday and said my rosary nightly. I went to school, graduated, got a job, didn't like it, got another. I enjoyed listening to music from Japan and I was a fan of Samurai movies. I got a first-degree black belt in Tae Kwon Do, I loved the Renaissance Fair. There was nothing unusual about my life or my interests—at least not until the middle of 2004, when my view on life was turned upside down.

My brother JP was busy working as a police officer in the city I was originally from. AP, a deputy sheriff, had just returned from a ghost hunting vacation in Gettysburg,

Pennsylvania, with his then fiancée (now wife). My father was in the hospital; he had another setback in his fifteen-year battle with cancer. By 2004, hospital visits were almost weekly. Most of the time he'd have to stay for days, sometimes longer. It would just be me and my mom home alone at night after visiting hours were over at the hospital. There was nothing unusual about that.

One night JP, AP, and his fiancée, decided to go to a Bastille Day festival taking place thirty minutes away. I didn't want to go. It was a hot and muggy night; I was more interested in staying home and enjoying my favorite television show, *Stargate SG-1*. JP was also a big fan and asked me to record the newest episode for him so he could watch when they got home. I went about my night, taking care of my pet rabbit and pet iguana. After a long day of running around the house, they were ready for dinner and then bed. As I put my iguana into her habitat, my mom decided she also was going to go and lie in bed and watch television for a while.

My show was almost on, so I quickly went around the house shutting off unnecessary lights—the living room lamps, the kitchen, and the light in AP's room, which he left on. I turned it off, leaving his door open behind me. I ran to the upstairs loft where my bedroom was and got into bed. I turned on my show, hit record, and enjoyed one of the best episodes I had seen. After the show ended,

I turned my television off and pulled the covers up to my chin, lying down to try to fall asleep. Just as my head hit the pillow, I heard what sounded like a door open and close, then heavy footsteps walking through the kitchen. It sounded like someone wearing boots. I assumed one of my brothers had come home. AP wore cowboy boots frequently, so I assumed it was him.

The footsteps sounded as if they were coming closer. I could hear the steps slowly clop past the stairs. Then, a door closed. It sounded as if it were in my brother's room. I went downstairs, assuming AP had come home and gone into his room. I wanted to know what the festival was like to see if I wanted to attend the next day. I saw through the crevice under the door that a light was on in the room. So I knocked. The door swayed open slowly on its own and showed me an empty room. The lights were on, but no one was home, so to speak. "Maybe he went to say goodnight to Mom," I thought. My brothers had a habit of waking my mom out of a deep sleep just to tell her goodnight. I went to my Mom's room. There she was sitting in bed still watching television.

"Who came home?" she asked.

"I don't know," I replied, realizing that obviously no one had come to see her.

"I thought I heard someone in the kitchen. Was that you?"

"No, I heard someone go into AP's room, and I thought he had come home. The light was on and I know I turned it off, so someone was in there." My next thought was that he had come home to get something and ran back out. I called JP's cell phone. When he answered, I could hear he was still at the festival.

"Is AP with you?"

"Yeah they're both here. Why?"

My mom and I looked at each other. We both heard someone in the house walking around with heavy footsteps. The festival was thirty minutes away, so if AP and JP were both there, it definitely wasn't them. I hung up on my brother after blurting out that someone broke into the house. Without thinking of what we were really doing, my mom and I bolted out of her room. She grabbed a butcher knife as my focus went on the basement door. I took a knife and stuck it in the door so if someone went down there, they couldn't get back up. I then grabbed a knife and started searching the house while my mom huddled on the couch. No one under the beds, no one in the closets, no one in the shower, no one…

I checked the front and side doors—they were both locked as they were all night. I went from window to window. Locked, locked, locked, locked, locked. Everything was as it should be. Nothing was tampered with; there was no way someone had gotten into that house.

My mom and I looked at one another. Were we sharing the same hallucination? How could two people, in two different rooms, on different levels of the house, have heard the same thing? I walked into my brother's room and turned off the lights. It was an old-fashioned switch. It was a heavy switch that would click loudly when you turned the lights on and off. There was no "in-between" where it could get stuck halfway down, and then pop back up. Off was off and on was on. When I turned the light off again, there was the telltale click. As I turned to leave the room …"CLICK." The lights were on!

I felt as if I were in a movie … the lights were starting to flicker as I turned back toward the light in slow motion. The switch was in the on position. I felt claustrophobic all of a sudden as I reached to turn the light off again. I pushed it down with a loud click, and held it there. I wanted to make sure it was as down as it could possibly be. The lights were off again. I started walking backwards to the door, my heart pounding. Thankfully, it seemed to be staying down. As I left the room, "CLICK" and the lights were on.

My brothers arrived home less than thirty minutes later. They must have been speeding to get there that fast. They searched the outside of the house. It had rained the night before, and the soft mud was sinking under their feet. They could see their footprints, but that was all they saw. There were no signs of anyone else around the house. JP never seemed to fully believe my mom and me, but AP and his fiancée had a different view. They had brought home a lot of little things from Gettysburg as souvenirs. Rocks, leaves they pressed in books, a little bit of dirt from the ground of a battlefield. AP's fiancée mused that perhaps a spirit followed them home. "Ridiculous," I thought to myself. "Ghosts don't travel...do they?"

I learned that they do indeed travel. A year after these events, I met Jason and Grant from *Ghost Hunters*, a show about paranormal investigation. They told me that many spirits attach to objects and will follow it wherever it goes. Some become attached to people while others roam from place to place until they find a spot they want to stay, much like we do in life. So a house that may not have been haunted before can become haunted under the right circumstances.

From that first night, strange things started happening. I'd hear my name being called. I'd ask who was looking for me, but no one would know what I was talking about. Things would tip over for no reason, I'd see shadows out of the corner of my eye. One night, I was on the phone with a friend. My remote control for the TV had stopped working, and I was complaining to her that I couldn't find all the extra batteries and how I didn't want to have to manually change the channel. We laughed at my laziness till something shot out of my closet like a bullet and hit my bed.

I screamed, but regained my composure and told my friend I would have to call her back. A box was tipped upside down on my floor right next to my bed. This box had been sitting on the top shelf of my closet for weeks. It wasn't precariously placed in there—I had it pushed all the way against the wall so it WOULDN'T fall off. Then I thought to myself, if it fell, it would land at the bottom of the closet floor, not eight feet away where my bed was. For it to fly eight feet, it would have to have been pushed or thrown. I slowly picked up the box, which spilled all of its contents. There, under the box, were the batteries I had searched everywhere for.

Not long after, my family was hit with a tragedy. May 11, 2005—my father passed away. It was expected, but unexpected at the same time. It took a long time after he passed for things to feel "normal" again. It was hard passing the room where he spent the last three years in a medical bed. The room was quiet without the loud hissing of his oxygen tank. His electric wheelchair sat motionless in the corner of the room.

One afternoon a month after he passed, my mom and I were shopping for groceries. After returning home, a light was blinking on the brand-new cordless phone we purchased a week earlier with a DIGITAL voice-mail machine. We didn't have caller ID, so I pressed play to hear the first person to leave a message on our new piece of technology. There was nothing but static, a sort of white noise. I thought the machine had malfunctioned. Then I heard something that made me stop in my tracks. I ran and got my mom and told her to listen. She heard the same thing. An hour later, JP came home on his lunch break and we made him listen. His jaw dropped. "Are you serious?" When AP came home we had him listen as well. We all heard it and it shocked us to the core.

It was Dad. It was his voice 100 percent, no doubt in our minds. Through the static, he simply said, "I love you." There was another voice on the phone that wasn't my dad's. It said something about "the light" but the message stopped abruptly. At that moment, so did the unusual activity in the house.

It made me question the paranormal. It made me wonder if there wasn't really a spirit in that found its way into my house, decided to stay knowing my father was ill and didn't have much more time left, and followed my dad when it was time to cross over to the other side.

After that moment, I saw things in a way I hadn't before. The paranormal was no longer an idle enjoyment; it was something I needed to know more about … I needed to understand. I contacted many people in the industry to learn as much as I could. From Noah Leigh of the Paranormal Investigators of Milwaukee (http://paranormal milwaukee.com), I learned about the various types of hauntings; residual, intelligent, demonic, and poltergeist. He told me how each different type of haunting could be identified.

I learned about different equipment used and how each piece of equipment is implemented; the K-II meter, the Mel meter, thermometers, video camera, etc. Armed with this information, I began my studies of the paranormal. My goals were to learn more about my experience, to help other with their experiences, and to try to answer the greatest question of all: Why? Why do ghosts haunt? What are spirits really? Why do they linger? Why? I armed myself with a K-II meter, a Mel meter, two Sony digital voice recorders, a Galileo High-Power Telescope, and several video cameras. I learned about each piece of equipment, their pros and cons, and set out.

And here is where the journey begins. A lone investigator roaming the country for answers.

two

Mission Point Resort

....

Most paranormal investigators agree that an intelligent haunting is a haunting caused by something with consciousness. You can ask for intelligent responses to questions or see if an object can be manipulated physically.
—Noah Leigh (Paranormal Investigators of Milwaukee)

The History

Mackinac Island is a beautiful getaway tucked between the bulk of Michigan, and Michigan's Upper Peninsula. It is a beautiful place right in our own backyards where one can escape the busy hustle and bustle of everyday life. Gone is the noise of tires squealing, horns honking, engines revving, motorcycles racing, and the clanking of tow trucks; no smell of gas, no fogs of oil burning, no traffic jams.

Motorized vehicles (with the exception of emergency vehicles) are not allowed on the island. In 1898, "horseless carriages" were banned from the island in fear they would spook the horses and put carriage riders and residents in danger. Even today, over one hundred years later, if you want to get around the island, you either take a horse-drawn carriage, rent a bicycle, or walk.

In the mornings on Mackinac Island, you are gently woken to the clip-clop of horse's hooves and the soft chimes of bicycle bells. Everyone has a friendly smile on their face as you pass them on the street. The smell of handmade confectioneries fills the downtown streets as you walk past the many fudge and candy shops. Watch as the masters of delectable delights make peanut brittle before your very eyes. If you love shoes and chocolate, Sanders Chocolatiers has the perfect souvenir for you; a life-sized pure chocolate high-heeled shoe.

No matter where on the island you go, you have an amazing view of the crystal waters of Lake Huron. Off in the distance, you can see the timeless beauty of the lighthouse as the waves crash against the rocks upon which it stands. At night, the pale moon casts a glow in the shimmering waters like a pool of magic. Across the great lake at night you may see lights of every color, like a Christmas tree, as a giant barge glides its way across the waters. All along the island are Victorian-era houses of every color, meticulously maintained to historical detail. Gardens gently lace the grounds of these homes with flowers of every hue, sending their fragrant scents into the air. Lilac bushes adorn the streets of the island and are honored every June with the lilac festival where there is food, friendly people, and the crowning of the lilac queen. Then, just when you think you have seen it all … on either end of the island rests the majestic and historical Grand Hotel and Mission Point Resort.

If you enjoy good movies, before visiting the island you must watch the romantic and passionate movie, *Somewhere in Time*, starring Christopher Reeve and Jane Seymour. The movie is about a playwright who falls in love with a photo of a beautiful woman from the 1800s while staying at the Grand Hotel on Mackinac Island. He finds a way to travel back in time to meet the mysterious woman of his dreams, an actress performing a play at the theater in the Mission Point Resort. The movie was filmed on the island. It was one of the extremely rare occasions that the "no motorized vehicles" law was lifted. They used cars in the film to show the time change from the modern era (modern in 1980) and the past. If you watch the movie, many things on the island are still the same, like the island is frozen in time.

The island was originally sacred land to the Anishinaabe (Ojibwa) tribes of Native Americans. They believed the island was the home of Gitche Manitou, the Great Spirit. The island was a gathering place for the tribes to meet and honor the Great Spirit with offerings and to lay their tribal members to rest when their journeys came to an end. Across the expanse of the island are unmarked sacred burial plots, which were left undisturbed for generations until the island started to become populated, and burial sites were uprooted during construction. Even as recently as the winter of 2011 during renovation to buildings, bones have been unearthed. When this occurs in modern times, arrangements are made with the Sault Ste. Marie tribe of Chippewa Indians to have a proper Native American ceremony to re-bury their ancestors with respect.

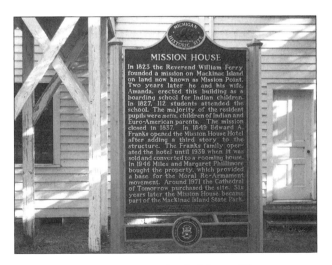

The historical marker for the Mission House.
Photo by Andrea Mesich.

In the 1820s, a missionary by the name of Rev. William Ferry came to Mackinac Island. There, he decided to build the legendary Mission House where he housed and educated Native American children. A few years later, he founded Mission Church. Both buildings still stand today, and because of these landmarks, the southeast section of the island is known as Mission Point.

One of the most interesting historical notes pertaining to Mission Point has to do with the resort's lobby. What is now the main lobby originally was constructed to be the world conference center for a group known as the MRA (Moral Re-Armament). The MRA was led by Dr. Frank Buchman, and existed to promote love, unselfishness, honesty, and purity among all nations. In 1954, the groundbreaking ceremony marked the beginning of what was meant to be a place for nations to come together in peace and harmony.

This structure was created in the form of a giant, thirty-six-foot high, sixteen-sided tepee constructed with majestic nine-ton tresses. It is said this tepee's construction fulfilled an ancient Native American prophecy. "*Someday, on the east end of the Island, a great tepee will be erected. All nations will come there and learn about peace.*"

The MRA eventually took the organization to Switzerland and deeded the property to what became the Mission Point College. The college lasted for only four years, from 1966 to 1970, just long enough to see one graduating class. The college sold the land to popular evangelist Rex Humbard who planned to turn the area into a spiritual and religious retreat. After two years, the retreat dissolved and eventually the area became home to what we now call Mission Point Resort. Of all places on the island, the most haunted is the area known as Mission Point. Mission House, Mission Church, and the Mission Point resort are all home to many spirits that wander the halls.

Not far from the Mission Point Resort is a small and seemingly unassuming pond that has been dubbed "the Drowning Pool." It seems so innocent, just a pretty pool of water near the "Bistro on the Greens," which rests on a golf course. However, appearances are deceiving; the middle of what appears to be a shallow pool actually reaches depths of over twenty feet. Because of its depths, this pond was the sight of a terrible tragedy of justice.

I spoke to a married couple who were regulars at Mission Point. They seemed to know a lot about the pond. As we ate truffle fries at the Bistro on the Greens restaurant, the couple told me the story of this unassuming water.

As the legend goes, in the 1700s, brothels were popping up all over the island. These places of sin with women of the night would lure soldiers who were stationed at Fort Mackinac, fur traders, and husbands. To avoid the stigma of being seen with these women of ill repute, the men who were caught with their pants down (so to speak) cried

"WITCH" much like the Salem Witch Trials that took place in Massachusetts in 1692–1693. Seven women stood accused of using witchcraft to lure these "innocent" men to commit an act of sin against their will. They were taken to the drowning pool to test their innocence. If they floated, they were witches and would be condemned to death. If they drowned, they were innocent. (Oops). So rocks were tied to the feet of all the women, and they were tossed into the deepest part of the pond. All seven drowned.

The drowning pool at Mission Point Resort.
Photo by Andrea Mesich.

It is said that the restless spirits of these women still roam the area, unable to leave because of the tragic events leading up to their deaths. They are bound to this place until they can overcome how they, innocent women, were condemned to die. In 2009, during a tour of the most haunted places on the island run by "Haunts of Mackinac," a group experienced the sorrow of the women. The entire group witnessed a black shadow cross over the pool and hover right above the center, where the women would have been tossed in to drown. After a few seconds of hovering there, the shadow disappeared, as if it fell into the center of the pool.

In 2011, another group on a haunted tour of Mackinac, all saw a large orb of light hovering over the pool. Not only did they all see it with the naked eye, some caught the image on camera. The most interesting thing about this orb, besides being seen with the naked eye, was that it seemed to cast its own light. In fact, you could see the light reflected in the water below it. It was more than merely an orb of dust or moisture, which are not visible to the naked eye, nor do they cast their own reflection on surfaces like water. Could these events, the shadow and the ball of light, be the spirits of the women, lingering in this world till they are properly proclaimed innocent? The couple believed it was more than possible, but could not be certain, not having witnessed any of the phenomena themselves. "There's a strange feeling there, but we've never seen anything."

In the 1800s, when Mission House was still active as a home and school for Native American children, many children took ill due to an outbreak of tuberculosis. These children developed high fevers and had trouble breathing. In an effort to ease the fevers, the children were placed in the basement. Unfortunately, the cold and damp basement only exacerbated their problems and sixteen children are said to have passed away from complications due to tuberculosis or pneumonia.

At this time, according to a tour guide from Haunts of Mackinac, Mission House is used as housing for Mission Point Resort employees. Although no children reside there now, the sound of children can still be heard—feet running up and down the hall when no one is there and the echoes of childlike laughter. Lights turn off and on without reason; occasionally, employees state they see children standing before them, then suddenly, they're not. Could the souls of these children who died from illness still be playing in the halls of Mission House?

The most famous spirits of Mission Point would be the ones known as Harvey and Lucy. Harvey wanders all over Mission Point Resort. From the main lodge to the straits lodge to the theater, he is seen, felt, and heard in many places. It would not be so odd for him to do so, since the whole resort was once his stomping grounds. You see, Harvey was a student when the resort was the college…and it was on the college/resort grounds that he died.

As the story goes, Harvey was a college student who had fallen in love with another student. The two had a whirlwind romance, and Harvey was extremely happy. In a very public display of love, Harvey got down on one knee and asked his girlfriend to marry him. His girl-friend's feelings were not as strong as his. She looked at their relationship as more of a fling than true love, and rejected his proposal outright. Depressed and heartbro-ken, Harvey allegedly took his life on the cliffs behind the college, which now overlooks the resort's pool area.

Harvey is said to still haunt the straits lodge, specifi-cally, the room that use to be his dorm. Those who have seen Harvey's apparition describe him as a tall and slender young man with brown hair, blue jeans, and a white T-shirt. He is said to be a practical joker, and a bit flirtatious with female guests. Females who sleep in his former dorm room will occasionally feel something or someone crawl-ing into bed with them at night. Many women say they feel phantom arms around their waist, or touching their arms. At times, they see imprints in the sheets of a body, as if someone was just lying there, when there shouldn't have been. In one case, there was a woman whose husband had gone to the bathroom. She felt someone climb in bed with her and put his arms around her. She assumed it was her husband until she heard the toilet flush.

Harvey seems to enjoy being a slight nuisance to the workers of Mission Point Resort. Employees have com-plained about cleaning a certain area of the resort, only to return and find things askew and in disorder, forcing them to clean the area again. Many times workers would put things up only to see them knocked down before their very eyes. These were practical jokes Harvey liked to play. Nothing Harvey has done is considered malicious or in ill spirit. He simply seems to enjoy playing little pranks and seeing the reactions.

Harvey is known to frequent the Mission Point Theater where some of *A Moment in Time* was filmed. He was known to enjoy the arts, and even participated in the theater back in the college days, so it is not unusual for him to join a few other spirits that are said to haunt the theater on occasion. Of all the places, the theater seems to get the most activity. The theater is actually a hotspot for many spirits. Another spirit that resides there is Harvey's friend, little Lucy.

Lucy is a little girl who is usually found playing in the theater at Mission Point Resort. More specifically, she seems to spend a lot of time in the balcony. Not much is known about Lucy—not even if that is her real name. A psychic who had investigated the theater gave her the name Lucy. However, was that her real name, or simply what the little girl wanted to be called? Was the psychic picking up on a name of another spirit who roams the theater, and attributed it to the little girl by mistake? No one knows for sure. Perhaps the little girl was trying to tell the psychic about someone else whose name was Lucy and the psychic misunderstood. There is no telling. We just do not know all the circumstances of what the psychic allegedly heard or saw. But Lucy stuck and that is what the little girl now responds to.

I ponder to myself if the little girl wasn't from just a few feet away at Mission House. Mission House is on the same property, basically a hop, skip, and jump away from the theater. Perhaps she was one of the sixteen children who died of complications from tuberculosis. Many spirits wander the island. Harvey himself goes between the main lodge, the straits lodge, and the theater. They are not stuck in one place. At the very least, it seems, they can move about a small area. While there are no documents of a child named Lucy living in the Mission House at the time children died, again, it could be possible her real name is not Lucy.

In the theater, people have heard a little girl giggling in the balcony; they've seen apparitions of a little child appear before their eyes and disappear just as quickly. Some investigators bring toys for her to play with. Many have seen the toys move on their own; sometimes they would leave their toys there for Lucy only to find them gone when they return. Sometimes the toys would eventually find their way back, sometimes Lucy liked them too much, and kept them.

There are more than a few ghosts that reside at Mission Point Resort, but the ghosts of Harvey and Lucy are the most famous and by far the most active; so active in fact, they garnered the attention of some very famous visitors.

Ghost Hunters is a groundbreaking reality show that made its television debut on the Syfy channel (then Sci-Fi) in 2004. The series follows the founders of "The Atlantic Paranormal Society" or TAPS, Jason Hawes and Grant Wilson as they and their top team of investigators travel the country (and sometimes the world) to explore the paranormal and find answers to the greatest mysteries. In each episode they help people at wits' end with paranormal problems, find answers to why ghosts haunt their homes or businesses, why the spirits still wander the earth, and try to learn answers to the paranormal world's greatest questions.

In season 7, episode 706, the TAPS team made its way to Mackinac Island to investigate the infamous Mission Point Resort. They were specifically there to investigate the hauntings of Harvey's room, and the theater where both Harvey and Lucy (as well as other spirits) are known to be most active. They found Mission Point quite interesting, and quite active. They were even able to uncover information about Harvey. He did exist, according to historical records the TAPS team were able to dig up in Mackinac Island archives. His name was not Harvey, but out of respect for surviving family members they did not release this information to anyone but Todd, the owner of Haunts of Mackinac, in private.

The Investigation

When preparing to investigate the reported hauntings of Mission Point Resort, the first thing I did was grab the book *Haunts of Mackinac: Ghost Stories, Legends and Tragic Tales of Mackinac Island* by Todd Clements. Brilliantly written, it contains stories of some of the most haunted locations of the island. Every nook, every cranny has a story to tell. There is the story of the Rifle Range Trail soldier along with a story of a servant girl who committed suicide in the early years of Stonecliffe Mansion. There is a woman seen at Post Cemetery weeping over graves. The book is so full of interesting and compelling ghost stories, I could not put it down. It raised my anticipation for seeing the island with my own eyes.

After seeing the segment on *Ghost Hunters*, I was most fascinated with Mission Point Resort and the alleged hauntings of Harvey and the little girl known as Lucy. On *Ghost Hunters*, many times Jason and Grant are able to find logical explanations for sights and sounds thought to be paranormal activity. However, the locations they determine could be haunted are the ones that pique my curiosity. One of those places happened to be Mission Point Resort.

After reading the wonderful book written by Todd Clements, I immediately emailed him, telling him of my curiosity about the resort and the alleged hauntings. Todd was gracious enough to extend to me a special invitation to the island, a free tour of the area as well as an opportunity to investigate the most active place on the island, the theater at Mission Point. Besides being the author of the fascinating and attention-grabbing *Haunts of Mackinac*, Todd also owns a business by the same name. The business is attached to Mission Point Resort near their deli. Haunts of Mackinac offers tours of the island's haunted downtown area through Mission Point Resort. If you don't like long walks, they offer a smaller Mission Point only tour. They also offer budding paranormal investigators a chance to investigate the theater. There is also a small gift shop.

Intrigued by the mystery of the island, I booked my room as soon as I had the chance. I made sure they gave me a room as close to Harvey's dorm as possible. I was able to secure the room 2365, just down the hall from 2345. The whole floor is said to be fairly active, so I was hoping I could coax Harvey into playing a practical joke on me in my room or interacting with me on some level. I wanted to have a better understanding of the alleged hauntings, and how those who experienced the hauntings felt at the moment.

On a mild day in June, I packed my bags and prepared to leave for the island. I brought my mom and my dogs along so they could enjoy a small vacation from the hustle and bustle of everyday monotony. They could wander and explore the island's many treasures while I explored the island's many mysteries.

We arrived in St. Ignace, Michigan, and hopped onto the Star Line Ferry headed to the island. Once I got off the ferry and took my first steps into downtown Mackinac Island, I was in awe. The streets were filled with smiling people walking from shop to shop. Old-fashioned carriages pulled by tall and strong horses drove down the streets taking passengers to and from the hotels, resorts, or bed and breakfasts. People on bicycles rode up and down the streets, the occasional tinkle of bells ringing to let people in the street know there was a bike behind them wanting to pass. And there were no vehicles in sight. Looking up and down the street, the downtown looked almost exactly as it had in the movie *A Moment in Time*. There were gift shops, fudge shops, clothing stores…I was speechless as I took everything in.

We arrived at Mission Point Resort, rounding the corner of a beautiful garden of flowers, with a beautiful view of Lake Huron. Mission Point Resort is one of the few hotels on the island that is dog friendly, which is a great plus for those who enjoy traveling with their beloved pets. As I walked into the main lobby to check in, I was greeted by a number of other guests with their dogs. My two couldn't have been happier as they took the time to say hello to their new friends. Inside the lobby was the legendary giant tepee that was prophesied long before it was even in the imagination of the architect. Everyone who worked at Mission Point Resort was extremely friendly. From the front-desk staff to the bellhops to the cleaning crew, no one would let you walk by without a friendly smile. You got the feeling that they truly loved their jobs.

I took my time walking from the main lodge to the straits lodge where we were staying. I wanted to get a feel for the whole area in the daylight. As my mom and I walked the dogs toward our hotel room, we passed the infamous theater where Harvey and Lucy are said to be more active. I stopped in front of the doors and looked at it for a while. My mom said it gave her a bad feeling and she didn't want to linger. My mom is not one to get spooked. She's a very levelheaded, rational person. So when she feels spooked (or as she calls it, "being creeped out"), my interest is even more piqued. Something may be there if it gets my mom nervous.

We took an antique-feeling elevator to Harvey's floor, and began to walk down the hall. As we passed room 2345, I stopped and looked at the door. I was willing Harvey to come out and interact with me. That night, after settling into the room, nothing seemed to happen. No knocks on the wall, no lights turning on and off—the only sounds were my dogs snoring by my feet.

After a day of shopping, sampling the various foods at various bistros, and walking my dogs on a path near the crystal-blue waters of Huron, I headed to the Haunts of Mackinac store next to the Lakeside Marketplace, attached to the side of Mission Point Resort where the main lodge is located. It was nearly time for the tour Todd had graciously set me up on. The store had a deliberately spooky feel to it. It was dark, lit only by black lights and neon lights of purples, dark reds, yellows, and blues. The fog machine rolled a light mist throughout the store, and a robed skeleton statue greeted you at the door.

The store is filled with merchandise. The book *Haunts of Mackinac* by Todd Clements, a video about Haunted Mackinac filmed by the Upper Peninsula Paranormal Society, LED-lighted necklaces, bracelets and pins of little ghosts, T-shirts, and paranormal investigative equipment such as the K-II meter. On the counter there are pictures of Mackinac Island, including a photo of what is believed to be an actual ghostly shadow, and a photo of Todd with Jason and Grant from *Ghost Hunters*. There was a lot to take in as I paced around the shop a bit. I bought a DVD, a T-shirt, a fun ghost LED blinking bracelet, and a pin.

I introduced myself to the tour guide of the Mission Point tour. She donned a black hooded cloak as she introduced herself to the other guests who had joined us for the tour. As dusk was creeping in, we set out. While there was a whimsy to the little shop and the tour with the black lighting and hooded cloaks…the tour was extremely professional, very informative. At times, the stories pulled out various emotions in all the listeners. The chilling tales, the history, the legends were extremely interesting to hear while looking at the very places being described.

We ended the tour in the theater. The tours were not allowed to take anyone backstage or into the balcony where a lot of the activity happens, but I knew my time to see those places was coming in just a few short hours. As she spoke about the history of the theater, I took a look around. It seemed relatively unassuming. I didn't get a sense of anything out of the ordinary. Even when the lights were off, it seemed like a normal theater in the dark.

From the theater the tour guide took us into the darkened soundstage. There we heard stories of people getting touched, scratched, people saw shadowed figures walking around, they heard phantom voice both male and female, and there was a report of someone who worked at the resort being pushed through doors while working in the soundstage after hours. One member of our tour spoke up and stated that she and her husband had investigated the soundstage before. She said it was one of the few places she felt extremely uncomfortable in. I didn't share in that particular feeling. It was curious. With all the stories of things that happened in that room, I felt nothing that would make me feel there was something there. I was looking forward to investigating the areas to see if I would experience anything myself or find reasonable ways to explain what happened to others.

The next day I spent the afternoon shopping, walking my dogs, sightseeing with my mom, watching people flying kites, and buying life-sized chocolate high-heeled shoes from Sanders Chocolatiers. Occasionally my mom and I would sit on a park bench and watch the seagulls tease my dogs. After a fun and relaxing day, it was time to get back to my room and prepare for the investigation that evening. I gathered the equipment I would be bringing with me: two digital audio recorders, a digital video camera, and a toy for little Lucy. "Haunts of Mackinac" would be providing the K-II meters. K-II meters are EMF readers (electromagnetic fields). The green light shows it's on, then there are various level of lights from yellow to red that shows the intensity of EMF in the area, whether man-made or natural. The theory is spirits can manipulate the EMFs around them in order to communicate. If you ask a question, you can ask a spirit to turn the lights on to red and keep it there, or to make the meter blink two times for yes and one time for no.

The evening of the investigation, I met lead investigator Cornelius Maki and fellow investigator Kimberly Cenci. While Cornelius got everything together and waited for the rest of the investigators, I had a chance to talk to Kimberly a little about the upcoming investigation. I asked a little more about Lucy, the little girl who haunts the theater. Kimberly shook her head. "Not much is really known about her. We don't even know if Lucy is really her name…the name came from when a psychic looked around the theater. Other than that, nothing is known about her." As I stated earlier, I theorized that perhaps the little girl was one of the children who died in the Mission House up the way. While there was no Lucy at the house, perhaps Lucy is not the child's name. It could be the name of another spirit there, perhaps Lucy was referring to someone else and not herself, or perhaps she gave herself a "stage" name since she was playing in the theater. One thing Kimberly did note was that "she seems to enjoy playing on the balcony, and usually enjoys the presence of women. If a man is around, she usually isn't very active." Kimberly thought for a second and corrected her thought. "Actually, there is one guy she seems to like, and that's Cornelius. He's the exception to the rule. He's been working here for so long, and sometimes he brings her little gifts to play with. Lucy responds to him."

I asked Kimberly if there were any other spirits in the theater besides Lucy and Harvey. She stated that there were a few other spirits throughout the Mission Point Resort. Another male entity and a female entity they identify as "The Opera Singer."

When the other investigators arrived for the night, Cornelius passed out glow stick necklaces for us to wear as a way to keep track of each other. If someone wasn't wearing the glow stick, they probably didn't belong there. I immediately cracked mine open and gave it a little shake to get the glow started. I placed it around my neck as Cornelius gave a few last-minute instructions before taking us in.

I followed Kimberly into the theater. It was very dark inside and took my eyes a little time to adjust as I headed down the aisle toward the stage. I placed my video recorder stage right and began recording the empty seats in the theater. Stage left, Cornelius set up an LED light grid that filled the entire theater with tiny green and red dots. The theory behind the light grid is that it makes entities easier to see. If an entity is able to manifest itself in the form of a person or shadow, that mass will pass in front of the beam and disrupt the flow of light. This in turn makes it easier to see potential entities.

Once the K-II meters had been passed out, everyone split up to cover more ground. The first place I wanted to check out was the balcony where little Lucy is said to play. Kimberly, and one other investigator joined me. Kimberly quickly pointed out the dangers of the balcony as a warning to be careful where we sat. "The railing is very low, and it just kind of drops off. In the dark, it's not safe; so try not to go further then this row." Heeding her warnings, I stayed back a few rows and placed my recorders in different spots on the balcony. I tested the area with the K-II meter to find any potential spikes in natural electromagnetic fields. When using equipment like a Mel meter or K-II meter, it's always good to do an area sweep. If you find random spikes or solid spikes in EMF, any potential hits you get during a K-II session would be questionable. Once I found no random spikes, I placed the K-II meter in front of me and found a chair in which I wanted to sit. I waited to see if the K-II would randomly spike. When nothing happened after a few minutes, I began seeking Lucy.

I called on the name of Little Lucy and asked her to come out and play. I tried to talk to her the same way I talk to my nieces and nephews. I tried to make things personal to make her comfortable. I told her who I was and how far I came just to play with her. I asked her questions about herself. If she liked playing with things people brought her, if she knew Harvey, if she and Harvey were friends. I noticed an empty drink can on the ground and asked if she was upset that people left litter in her balcony. I took out the blinking LED bracelet I bought from the gift shop and showed her how it turned on and off and told her she could play with it if she wanted to. I placed it a few chairs away and asked if she could turn it on. No answer seemed to come. The K-II didn't spike at all, and I didn't feel any unusual presence; it was quiet.

After snapping a few photos, Cornelius called out for everyone to join him in the first row of the theater seats near the stage. I grabbed my recorders and walked down the balcony stairs. He stated that anyone who had not been to the soundstage was welcome to join him there now. Those who were already there, as well as a few others who were originally backstage, decided to join Cornelius. I was the only one who stayed behind in the theater to continue my investigation. I decided I wanted to see if I could get Harvey to communicate with me.

I sat in Harvey's special chair. The chair was like all the others, except for a notch in the seat where a chunk of wood was missing. The chair squeaked as I gently pushed it down so I could take a seat. It was like any of the other chairs. The odd thing was, the longer I sat, the closer the room felt—an almost claustrophobic feeling, and I am not usually claustrophobic.

Harvey's chair in the theater at Mission Point Resort.
Photo by Andrea Mesich.

I started trying to communicate with Harvey. I placed my recorders in the row where I sat, and the row behind me. I started by telling Harvey a little about myself. When I told him who I was and why I was there, I asked him to tell me something about him. "You can just tell me one word. If you're lonely, say 'Lonely,' or if you're a practical joker say 'funny.' I want to know." Nothing immediately seemed to happen, so I tried a different angle. I asked him about his girlfriend who broke his heart. I sympathized with him, telling him I had a relative who had a girlfriend by the same name. They recently broke up as well. I asked if he was upset when he saw couples coming into the theater, or if he still had feelings for his girlfriend.

As I continued asking questions, it felt as if the seat was starting to shake. Even the chairs next to me seemed to be vibrating. I tried to think of what could be causing this. Perhaps air was pushing through the vents or some sort of mechanical system was turning on. I didn't hear anything different than what I had heard all night, yet the vibrating was intensifying.

Kimberly suddenly walked into the theater after leaving the sound room, and immediately, the vibrating stopped. She excitedly told me how they were doing an EVP session and everyone heard an audible "SHUT UP." It was an exciting moment since everyone had heard the sound and corroborated each others experience. Only true paranormal investigators get excited over phantom voices telling them to be quiet. She asked if anything odd happened while I was alone, explaining that the last time she sat in the chair, the chair started vibrating…this verified my experience before I even had the chance to tell Kimberly about it.

After a few minutes, Cornelius and the others returned to do a group EVP session in the theater. We sat on a seat in the front row, Cornelius sitting on the floor in front of us. Going down the line, we each took a turn asking a question of the spirits that may be in the theater. After everyone had a chance to ask a question, we wrapped up the EVP session and once again decided to check out the area of our choice. We all seemed to gravitate to the soundstage since there was a shared experience earlier. We hoped it would repeat itself.

I followed the group to the soundstage. I was curious if I could hear the same "Shut up!" or sounds of knocking or anything else others had been experiencing that night. I walked around a bit, placed my recorders in a few different spots, and listened carefully to someone who was asking EVP questions. I asked a few of my own, but while others said they felt various things (being poked, cold spots, a sense of foreboding), I honestly didn't feel anything. The only thing I really sensed all night was in Harvey's chair, and while the vibrating was weird—how it started and then stopped as soon as Kimberly entered the room—I couldn't say with any certainty that it was paranormal and not some kind of ventilation system kicking in. I looked around the room at the reactions of others and wondered: *Are they feeling what they think they're feeling, or feeling what they believe they should be feeling based on the stories they heard?* The power of suggestion.

As I looked around, I noticed Kimberly and Cornelius speaking in low voices to one another. Cornelius looked extremely pale and slightly disturbed. Kimberly had a look on her face that gave away her surprise. While I couldn't make out what they were saying, I could tell he was upset about something. Being a bit nosy, I went over and asked if everything was all right. He seemed a bit hesitant to say anything. He seemed worried that what he was about to tell me was so beyond belief, I would probably think he was crazy. I assured him that I would take what he had to say very seriously, so he started to explain what happened.

He showed me his recorder. It was the state-of-the-art model, perfect for collecting electronic voice phenomenon with its vast amount of storage and strong internal mic with an outlet to attach an external mic. I had my eye on a similar model, but it was out of my price range. I had seen him with it earlier when we did our group EVP session. He had picked it up, rewound the audio to see if anything audible had been collected during the session, but when nothing was heard, stated he would listen to the audio on his computer later. He tried to explain what happened, but decided instead to show me.

He gently held his recorder in the palm of one hand, and easily removed the casing with the other. The recorder fell apart. Cornelius explained that he was on his way back to the soundstage, holding the recorder in his hand trying to capture any potential sounds on the way back. He stopped when he thought he felt something, and suddenly he saw his recorder lift several inches out of his hand, hover, then slowly rest back down in his hand, only to immediately fall apart. That's when he noticed that all of the screws that held the casing together were missing. Not just one, not two, not even three … all of them. I looked closely at the recorder and he was right. All of the screws were gone. It didn't make sense. I can see one or two screws coming loose and falling apart, but every screw? Plus, he mentioned that the recorder was relatively new, so the screws should not have been that loose. And how strange was his story that it lifted out of his hand, hovered, and was slowly placed back in his hand, sans screws?

I could tell by the look on his face and the sound of his voice, what he experienced was very real and he was not exaggerating. He was as perplexed as I was, and it had happened to him. It was a very strange occurrence indeed. Everyone else, unaware of what Cornelius had been through, continued looking around the soundstage. I was curious to move on to the backstage area. It is said that a marine was so frightened by what happened to him while investigating the backstage area all alone that he left the theater and refused to come back, even though his wife stayed. Cornelius said he would show me the way.

On the way from the soundstage to the backstage, Cornelius stopped a few minutes to search the ground where the recorder incident happened to see if he could find any screws. Not successful, we continued backstage. I placed my audio recorders in a few different places. Cornelius, sitting down, held his recorder together, then gently placed it in front of him on the ground. The recorder still worked since only the outer casing fell apart. I sat down on the floor and looked around.

I once again started asking to speak with Harvey. I tried to once again sympathize with his woeful love life. I reminded him of the story I told him about my relative who had broken up with a girl by the same name as the woman who broke his heart. I told him that I, myself, was single and unlucky in love. I jokingly said, "Maybe I'm too picky and you're not picky enough. Maybe that's our problem." There seemed to be no response. I tried daring Harvey to touch me in some way. Poke me in the arm, tug on my sleeve, pull my hair a little; play a practical joke on me. Do something to interact with me.

I heard Cornelius rewind his recorder and put it to his ear. He did that several times with a look of concentration on his face. Cornelius could only say, "Whoa, you have to hear this," as he moved closer and rewound the tape again. He held it closer to my ear, and I could hear it very clearly. As I'm asking Harvey to do something to make himself known, like play a practical joke on me…there is a male voice whispering over my own voice…"Get out." He played it again, and it was definitely "Get out." It seemed oddly aggressive. It made me wonder, was this Harvey's idea of a practical joke…or was this a different spirit—the one who told everyone in the soundstage to "shut up" earlier? I quietly hoped I caught it on my own recorder. Cornelius asked, for good measure, if the entity could say it again for me. Shortly after, I took out my K-II and asked whatever was with us to show themselves by making the meter light up. It spiked once. I uttered, "that was weird" because it was only once, and then nothing.

Cornelius took off his glow stick necklace and placed it on the ground between us. "Whoever is here," he said, "make that glow stick roll, even just a few inches. A few feet would be even better, but do something." We sat there and stared at the glow stick, glowing eerily on the stage. We were almost willing it to move. Nothing happened. We waited a few more minutes and decided nothing was going to happen. Cornelius picked his glow stick up and placed it back around his neck as I gathered my recorders.

We started walking when a strange noise caught our attention. It was coming from this closet-like area near a wall ladder that led up in the rafters. Cornelius called out "Is someone there?" but no answer came. As we walked a little closer to the dark closet, a flash of light dropped from directly above and fell straight down onto a tarp inside the closet with a loud THUD, taking us both by surprise. Suddenly I heard running up in the rafters and what sounded like a snicker. Immediately, Cornelius turned on a light so we could see, and bolted up the ladder into the rafters. "No one is up here," he called down in a frantic voice. "This is NOT possible. There is no one up here at all!"

I asked if there was another way down. Cornelius opened a trap door right next to the ladder he climbed up. "This is it," he stated. There were only two ways down … to fall through the trap door, which would have been a dangerous jump in the dark, into that closet where the glow stick fell … or to climb down the ladder immediately next to the trap door, where Cornelius climbed up. Either way, the only way out was to pass us. He closed the trap door with a heavy thud. I mused to myself that it could not have been the trap door. With no way down except to jump, they wouldn't be able to close the door behind them … and not only did I not hear a thud, the door was definitely closed when Cornelius climbed up.

Cornelius used the ladder to come down from the rafters, looking as confused as ever. He picked up the glow stick from the closet. "Someone has to be messing with us," he murmured under his breath. "This just isn't possible." I asked him what his thoughts about the glow stick were. He held it up to me. "This glow stick is not attached to a necklace. We should all have a necklace around our necks. If we go back and find that everyone has their glow stick, then we have a problem. These glow sticks last maybe twenty-four hours if you're lucky. They usually begin to dim way before then. So if we all have our glow sticks, this particular one shouldn't be glowing.

If this was from a recent tour (although most tours are not allowed backstage), then it would be dim, if not out. If it were from the last investigation, it would be out completely. Either way, this looks like a freshly cracked glow stick, which isn't possible. Then there is another issue. We do not usually take tourists up to the rafters, nor do we allow them to go up there when they are investigating on their own. So how would it have gotten up there? It makes no sense. The only thing I can think of is someone here is playing a joke. We need to check everyone to see if they have their sticks."

Before we headed back to the soundstage where everyone else was still investigating, making an exception, Cornelius allowed me to head into the rafters with him. I looked around and noticed that he was correct; the only way down I could see was the trap door, which was heavy, and the ladder which no one would have had time to run down even if I wasn't watching the area like a hawk, because Cornelius was up there before you could say boo. There was no way anyone could have escaped unnoticed. I looked around and found no one hiding. It boggled my mind. Since I could not explain the who, I wanted to try to explain the how. I found an area directly above the closet where the glow stick fell, and looked for a way it could have fallen down. I could not explain that either. I looked all around the floor. There were no spaces large enough to fit a glow stick. No loose floorboards that could be moved aside to push the glow stick through; no holes in the floor-boards that it could have fallen through. There was no explanation to how the glow stick got up there, how it got down, or who was in charge.

I climbed back down and asked if Cornelius could try to re-create the glow stick falling. Cornelius did a test to see if he could mimic the way the glow stick fell straight down by tossing it in various ways from the trap door. No matter how he tossed it, he could not replicate what we saw. It always flew from the side, then straight down, or fell from an angle and landed in different places. He could never get it to appear like it was falling straight down from the rafters, and I had already concluded there was no way to do that due to lack of openings the stick could have fit through above that closet.

Cornelius climbed down once again and I watched as he placed the still brightly lit glow stick in his pocket. He informed me that we needed to get the whole group together and do a glow stick check. He led the way back to the soundstage where everyone else was still investigating. I could see the faint trace of the glow stick glowing still in his pocket. As we walked, Cornelius kept repeating that "this can't be happening," and "someone has to be messing with us." Once we reached the soundstage, we gathered everyone into a circle and checked each person for their glow sticks. They all had them; I had mine, and Cornelius had his. Cornelius reached into his pocket. "You guys have to see this," was all he could say before his face went pale.

I saw Cornelius put his hand in his other pocket, then back in the first. He looked at me silently, and I looked back at him and simply said, "I saw you put it in your pocket, I even saw it glowing in your pocket!" I retraced our steps to see if I could find the glow stick. Could it have fallen out of his pocket? With me following behind, you would think I would have seen it fall or heard it when it hit the cement floor leading toward the sound room. Still, I looked under every nook and cranny to see if I could find the glow stick. It was nowhere to be found. It disappeared as mysteriously as it had appeared. I started to wonder if the glow stick was a ghost itself.

Cornelius decided since the group was all together again, we should go backstage and do a K-II session. I once again headed back to the location of the glow stick incident and placed my recorders down. We tested the area to see if we would get any spikes from natural EMF. We tested each other to make sure we weren't carrying anything that would create a natural EMF; then we waited to see if there were any random spikes.

Once we were confident there was nothing in the area or on us that caused spikes, we began to ask questions of any potential spirits in the area. I asked if it was Harvey that played the little joke with the glow stick. There was no answer on the meters. One other member of the group asked if perhaps the joke was played by the little girl named Lucy. The lights on all of our meters lit up to red and stayed there for a full second before turning off. I asked if she was trying to impress us, and once again the light lit up as far as the lights would go on the meter, then turned off.

The K-II meters were acting as if in direct response to questions. If we said nothing, the meters did nothing. If we asked a question and there was no response, perhaps the response was no. If we asked a question and the meter lit up, then perhaps the answer was yes. It was more than simply random. As I stated before, it was as if they were lighting up in direct response to questions. Many paranormal societies do not see much merit in K-II meter results, however, what I was seeing with the meters at this time made me question skeptics. While I would not rely solely on the K-II because you can miss so much if you are paying too much attention to the lights, and while there is a risk of false hits due to natural EMF…sometimes things are too "on" to call merely random or coincidence. If it were coincidence, then it was a repeated and odd coincidence, at least in my opinion.

Making the K-II session even more compelling, whenever the lights on the meter would light up as if answering a question, I felt a tugging on my sleeve as if someone was trying to catch my attention…however no one was even standing close enough to even accidentally brush up against my arm. Everyone else was standing across from me.

We once again asked if Lucy was still with us, and the meter lit up to red. When we asked if Harvey was with Little Lucy, the meters did nothing. We asked Lucy if she was alone—and once again, nothing. When we asked if Lucy had a friend with her, the meters lit up again. Someone asked if it was the opera singer perhaps; the meter lit all the way up again. When we realized the other spirit with Lucy was perhaps the opera singer, I asked if they wanted us to sing for them. The answer came on my meter alone, as if pointing me out.

I began to sing an aria from the opera *Madame Butterfly*, and as I sang, everyone's K-II meter not only lit up to the last red light, it stayed lit the entire time I was singing. They only turned off once I had completed the aria. I tried to sing another aria from *Faust*, however nothing happened on the meters at all. When I asked if perhaps they enjoyed *Madame Butterfly* more, the meters lit up. Again, it was lighting up too specifically to be coincidence. Once again, every time the meter lit up, I felt a tugging at my sleeve as if someone was trying to get my attention. A few times I brushed my arm and the tugging stopped, only to start up again.

It was past the end of the investigation's usual time, so we all started to pack up. I handed Cornelius back the borrowed K-II with a thank you for its use, and grabbed my own equipment. I turned off the recorders and packed them in my case. I went to get my video camera, which I had left on the stage, only to find the battery drained. That was curious. I had charged the battery completely, and had enough free memory to not only have lasted through the investigation, but even for another two hours. I would have to charge the battery later and see just how much I was able to capture on camera before it shut down, if anything.

Kimberly and Cornelius walked me back to the straits lodge, braving the swooping bats feasting on the bugs around the island. It was no wonder that, in a year when the biting flies and mosquitoes were seemingly plentiful, the island was relatively bug-free. The night was gone and we were creeping on the early hours of the morning. I would be leaving for home in just a few short hours, so I fell asleep the second I laid my head upon the pillow in my room.

The next morning, I reluctantly packed my things, got my dogs, and my mom and I boarded the ferry back to the mainland. I reached home to review the evidence I had found.

The Evidence

I started with the video camera. Once I had a chance to charge the battery enough to turn it on to upload the video, I found that the battery didn't even last twenty minutes, and during the twenty minutes that did record, the video was grainy and having a hard time focusing. The video was fairly useless to me, so I set it aside and hoped that I found something on audio. I was perplexed by the camera's battery running out. I know I charged it fully; I bought a memory stick with enough memory to last an entire investigation, and then some. I tested all of my equipment and everything was in working order. I have used the camera before and have used it since—and this was the first and only time this has happened.

The one thing that is worth mentioning, it is believed in the paranormal community that when a spirit manifests, it takes energy from wherever it can gather it. Sometimes that energy comes from batteries, and the batteries quickly drain when equipment is in use, as a spirit tries to manifest, causing equipment to power off. Could this be what happened in the case of my video camera? Could the focus have been malfunctioning because it was trying to focus on something that was there, but wasn't; then the battery drained as whatever it was tried to manifest? Due to the lack of useable video, I will never know for sure; I can only suspect.

There was a lot of audio to go through on my two recorders, and my way of reviewing evidence is to go over everything several times with a fine-tooth comb. When reviewing evidence, I do not ever want to leave one stone unturned. If I hear something, I want to hear it several times. I isolate the sound and listen to it in a loop, then I want to hear the entire clip and how it relates to the events around it. If it doesn't seem to fit, I put it aside and listen to it again later. If it is something I still cannot explain by natural means, I will ask paranormal investigators I trust who are experienced in EVPs to weigh in. Perhaps they have an idea I didn't think about. Once I have exhausted all efforts to explain what I have heard or seen, I then put it in the pile of potential evidence captured on an investigation.

I made a big pot of coffee and uploaded the audio to my computer. I got my trusted pair of headphones (over the ear headphones with a sound booster). When my laptop is at full volume, it amplifies the sound even more to make it easier to hear potential EVPs. I uploaded the audio to an audio program so I could easily tag any potential sounds I will want to review later, and got straight to work. It didn't take long for surprises to arise.

I listened to my EVP session when I was alone in the theater, sitting in Harvey's chair. I heard myself make a note out loud of the vibrating of the chair, but I did not hear any source of the vibration. No low hums or whirring of machinery or vents activating. I heard Kimberly come into the theater and tell me about the "shut up" incident. As we turned our conversation to the chairs vibrating, I heard a deep, male voice say loudly as if sitting right next to us, what I could only describe as the word "stroking." There were no men in the theater with us at that moment, and the word was so out of place, it didn't fit what was happening at that moment. I was not sure if the word being said was stroking, it could have been "spoken" or perhaps a word in another language. The thing I did know…it was a deep male voice…a voice that should not have been there. It was a voice neither Kimberly nor myself reacted to. It wasn't like we heard a voice and said "What was that?"; it was only upon playback that the voice was heard. Could I have captured Harvey? Or perhaps, was it one of the other nameless male spirits known to frequent the theater? Whichever the answer, it was a voice that should not have been there and that I could not explain.

I continued listening to the audio. I came to the point shortly after that moment we held the group EVP session. Each of us was able to ask a question. Our hope was that perhaps the spirits would respond to one of our questions, or perhaps feel more comfortable with a certain person. Listening to the audio, you could hear each voice, the tone, the quality, the inflections in the voices; the voices also sounded distant based on where the recorders were placed in relation to where we were sitting. Suddenly, as we asked questions, you could hear a loud and audible voice; a voice that sounded close to the microphone as it sounded louder than any of us asking questions sounded. It was a childlike female voice that sounded like she was saying, "Kick the can!" I was surprised.

I listened to the audio over and over. I isolated the sound, I played the entire clip, it was unexplainable. The voice did not match a single person who spoke during the EVP session. It was too close to the mic compared to any of our voices, and it was the voice of a child. Children have a certain inflection in their voice they lose as they become adults. Even an adult female with a higher-pitched voice still sounds like an adult. We lose a certain childlike quality in our voices after puberty. Even if you were able to find that one adult with a child's voice, that adult was not in our group. What was being said also did not make sense. We were speaking about names, and asking if anyone shared a name with one of the spirits in question. So "Kick the can" sounds out of place. One thing did make sense however. When I first investigated the balcony, there was that empty drink can someone left up there and I did ask Little Lucy if it made her mad that people littered her balcony. Later, someone pointed out that, especially in the era it is believed Lucy lived, kick the can was a popular child's game. This wouldn't be the last time I'd hear this same little girl's voice.

Not long after this incident, I found myself backstage with Cornelius, trying to call on the name of Harvey. Shortly after we began our EVP session, Cornelius caught the sound of "get out" on his recorder. The sound was clear. It was a male voice that sounded nothing like the one I had caught earlier. This voice sounded more annoyed, more gruff. The voice I heard earlier gave the feeling of being more friendly. Could this be the spirit that told everyone in the soundstage to shut up? Unfortunately, the sound did not appear on my recorders, I was only able to capture the sound when Cornelius was playing the sound back on his recorder. Cornelius asked whatever spirit said that so loudly on his recorder to do it again on mine. That's when I heard a small voice asking, "Why?" it was the voice of a child, the same female child who said "kick the can" earlier. It was such a small and innocent voice, asking why we would want someone to say "Get out" on my recorder.

I then heard myself place my K-II meter in front of me and ask whatever was with us to make the meter light up so we would know they were there. Suddenly I heard a male voice again, but not the one that said, "Get out." This was a different, kinder voice saying in a whisper, "the child is gone." After the whisper I can be heard saying "that was weird," as the K-II meter spiked for the first time backstage. Could this once again be Harvey, the one who said what I assumed was "stroking" or "spoken"? What did he mean, the child is gone? Perhaps the little girl who I assume is Lucy who said "kick the can" and "why" ran off. Could she have been chased off by the spirit that said "Get out"? Maybe "get out" was aimed at her, and not at Cornelius and I.

After I heard "The child is gone," nothing else happened until we came to the glow stick incident. When Cornelius ran up the ladder to see what was going on, I heard myself utter excitedly, "That was weird but cool." As I called up to Cornelius to ask him if there was any other way down, you could hear the same male voice that said "The child is gone" say "You're welcome, anytime," as if to say, "Glad I could do something cool for you."

During the K-II meter session, we asked if the glow stick was thrown by Harvey; you could hear me say that nothing happened on my meter. So another investigator asked if it was Lucy. We all acknowledged that our meters lit up. I asked if she were maybe trying to impress us by throwing the glow stick. I suddenly hear a very little whisper of a child saying "Yes!" almost excitedly. A second after the yes, everyone once again said the K-II meter lit up.

There were a few interesting things about these particular EVPs. They were no live reactions to the EVPs. They were loud enough that, if it were a person in the group, someone would have heard and replied…however they went unnoticed until the EVPs were played back. There was the voice of a child when no children were present in the building. When the male voice saying "stroken" or "spoken" occurred, the only people in the room were me and Kimberly. Everyone else was in the soundproof soundstage. The voices were the same. When I played the three clips that sound like a little girl back to back, it sounds like the same little girl. When I put a few of the male clips together, there were three that sounded the same ("stroken," "the child is gone," and "you're welcome: anytime"), and one that sounded different, a little harsher. This leads me to believe this is more than random sounds.

Many of the voices seem to coincide with hits on the K-II meter, which leads me to believe the hits on the K-II meter were not simply random. Some of the voices seemed closer to the mic than even my own voice. Having the recorders in my sight at all times, I know that no one went up to them to speak into the mics. This leads me to believe the voices were not voices belonging to any actual person.

Other sounds were captured…laughter, faint yells, and others that seemed out of place at the moment they were happening. However, these were the clearest, class 1 EVPs. There were also many personal experiences. The feeling of tugging on my sleeve, the glow stick that shouldn't have been glowing, that fell from a place it shouldn't have been able to fall—where it shouldn't have even been in the first place. Then when placed in his pocket, the same glow stick disappeared from his pocket. Plus the incident where Cornelius's recorder rose from his palm, and fell apart the moment it touched back down into the palm of his hand. There was also the vibrating of the chairs.

When I looked at the history of the island, the hauntings that occurred from one end of the island to the other, when I hear the stories of people who have had eerily similar experiences, when I think of my own experiences, and the experiences of the TAPS team in the episode "Frozen in Fear"…I leave the island with the feeling there is something going on there that can't be easily explained.

If you are not a believer in ghosts, I would recommend going to Mackinac Island. Visit the "Haunts of Mackinac" store and sign up for a tour. If you're even braver, sign up for a midnight investigation of the theater. Witness for yourself what lies on the island after the sun sets and the lights turn off. Will Harvey get into bed with you in the straits lodge of Mission Point Resort? Will little Lucy come play with you in the balcony of the theater? Or will there be something else that greets you, something not as happy to see you, telling you to get out, and get out now?

three

The Paulding Lights

....

EVP = electronic voice phenomenon. It is believed the reason we rarely hear spirits around us in person is because spirits speak to us on a different wavelength. It is believed that it takes the spirit less energy to speak through the recorder, which gives us a chance to hear what we may not otherwise hear, after the fact.

The History

On a long dirt road in Paulding, Michigan…a mystery unfolds on a nightly basis. A mystery that has gone unanswered for generations. The Paulding Lights have been luring people like a siren's song for decades. The ghost lights take place in Paulding on the border of Watersmeet in Michigan in the neighboring counties of Ontonogan and Gogebic.

Watersmeet, Michigan, has a vibrant and long history, as colorful as the fall leaves on the millions of acres of trees that encompass it. It is a beautiful area of the great northern woods of the Upper Peninsula resting between hundreds of crystal-blue lakes and quiet streams. The waterfalls sparkle as they fall into the rapids below; the stars in the night sky shimmer over the campers resting in Watersmeet's vast wilderness.

Watersmeet is a township in Michigan's Gogebic County in the Upper Peninsula. According to the book, *Public and Local Acts of the Legislature of the State of Michigan* (pre-1900s) the township of Watersmeet, Michigan, was founded in 1887 in Gogebic County (which organized in 1867) and the first election for the township chairs was held shortly after. So Watersmeet has well over a century of history in the great northern woods. Long and colorful histories make the perfect environment for ghost stories. Places with the most history seem to hold on to memories of the past. Sometimes, people who helped create those memories remain behind.

Even as places change, people move, new people come in, some things remain, unable to let go of the past. Whether it is a spirit that cannot let go of something he or she loved in life, or can't leave a place for whatever reason, or if it is a residual energy replaying a moment in time indefinitely, the longer and more intense the history, the greater the chance of a haunting.

Watersmeet was given its name because it is literally the place where waters meet. The Ontonagan River in Watersmeet, flows to meet Lake Superior. The Wisconsin River meets the Mississippi River, and the Paint River runs into Lake Michigan. There are approximately 302 lakes in or around Watersmeet, and nearly 300 miles of trout streams.

There are millions of acres of untouched nature in the Ottawa National Forest, and Watersmeet is in the heart of that forest. People come from all over for the beauty in that forest. There is something for everyone who enjoys the great outdoors—everything from hunting, to camping, ATV trails, snowshoeing, cross-country skiing, and kayaking. It is also the prime place for nature hikes, seeing the fall leaves change color, observing all kinds of wildlife, and viewing waterfalls. It is a nature lover's paradise. This land draws campers and hikers from all over the country, and in fact, other parts of the world.

Not long ago, I met a couple from Osaka, Japan, who had come to see the fall leaves in the beautiful forests. There was a couple from Canada who came to see all of the waterfalls, and do nature hiking. There was a family from Scotland visiting relatives in the Upper Peninsula who came to enjoy a little fishing and bird-watching. All who I met in my time studying the Paulding Lights, came to see the beauty this untouched patch of nature has to offer. Many also come for the fun offered at the Lac Vieux Desert casino.

The Lac Vieux Desert Tribal Band reside in Watersmeet, Michigan. In the year 1880, the Lac Vieux Desert Band made their home in the south shore of the Lac Vieux Desert, a lake that divides Gogebic County in Michigan, and Vilas County in Wisconsin. Lac Vieux Desert Lake is a sportsman's dream. The lake is home to bass, walleye, panfish, and home to the record-breaking tiger muskie. He was over 52 inches long and was 51 pounds, 3 ounces. However breathtaking the lake, it is the casino that attracts the most people.

Some skeptics of the Paulding Lights have attributed the legend to being a way to draw people to the casino—nothing more than a promotion to sell souvenirs and pull people in for some gambling. This theory has a few problems. The first problem, casinos in the Upper Peninsula and the bordering state of Wisconsin are extremely popular and do well already. The second problem is the casino does not sell Paulding Lights souvenirs, and the third problem with that theory is that the casino opened in 1996…thirty years AFTER the first documented sighting of the Paulding Lights. With the lights having preceded the casino by three decades, it would be false to say the legend was created as a gimmick for the casino.

The ghost lights, themselves, happen in a small, unincorporated town of Paulding in Ontonagan County, just on the border of Watersmeet, Michigan. If you're looking for historical information on the town of Paulding, it is not going to be an easy feat. When looking for information on the town, you'll usually be directed to sites pertaining to the lights themselves, or you will be taken to sites about Watersmeet. In fact, Paulding is so small that, if you're not careful, you may accidentally drive right on through and miss the town completely.

Paulding, Michigan, is in the heart of the Ottawa National Forest. Just east of Paulding is another popular site for tourists to delight in: Bond Falls. Bond Falls is a spectacular waterfall with a drop off at 40 feet high and more than 100 feet wide. It has been deemed one of the most picturesque waterfalls in all of Michigan. Not a small feat considering the number of waterfalls in the great northern woods from northern Wisconsin to the Upper Peninsula. To get to Paulding, you could take US Highway 45 north out of Watersmeet, or south out of another small town known as Bruce Crossing.

If you want to view the lights, you need to simply follow these directions. Take Highway 45 north out of Watersmeet, Michigan, for about five miles. Watch out as the road slowly bends to the right. On the left side, there will be a road called "Robbins Pond Road." (Some GPS systems have it down as Old Hwy 45.) There is usually a park sign right before the turn, on the right-hand side of Highway 45, so keep your eye out for it. When you see a sign to your right that says "Robbins Pond Road," make your left turn. You will know you are on the right road when you see a sign near the entrance that states the road is not a through street. If you travel up Robbins Pond Road a short ways, you will eventually come to a barricade where you can no longer go farther. This barricade is where you will stand to view the Paulding Lights come the setting of the sun.

This is the barricade on Robbins Pond Road where people stand to view the lights. Photo by Andrea Mesich.

Around a half mile to a mile away, there is a second barricade sectioning off part of the road that has been closed due to constant damage from heavy rains. There is also a stream that runs through the area. This road is the main reason the Paulding Lights have gotten a second name. Robbins Pond Road is an unimproved rural lane once part of a military road authorized by Abraham Lincoln during the Civil War in anticipation of a British attack through Canada. That swampy military road was originally called

Dog Meadow Road, thus earning the Paulding Lights the second name, "Dog Meadow Lights."

If you travel up Robbins Pond Road, you will find yourself surrounded on both sides by the vast Ottawa National Forest. Be sure to listen to the sounds of the trees rustling…is that a bear in those woods? A coyote? A raccoon? Or could it possibly be the ghost who is the source of the infamous Paulding Lights?

The Legends

The first documented sighting of the infamous Paulding Lights occurred in 1966. A group of teenagers was parked on an old stretch of military road once called Dog Meadow. After a short time, they saw a light coming toward the car, and within seconds the car was enveloped in a light unlike any they had ever seen. Before they could even comprehend what was going on, another light came dancing toward them. Terrified, the teenagers backed the car down the road, trying to get away, only to see the lights were still chasing them! The farther away they seemed to get, the closer the light seemed to be. They finally got off of the road, back onto the main street, and headed straight for the police department. They excitedly reported the incident to the police, though I wonder how seriously the officers took them. A car of teenagers being chased by balls of light? I'm sure most police officers back then would have looked at it as a practical joke.

Although this was the first documented sighting of the Paulding Lights, that does not mean there haven't been others. This is merely the first time someone reported their experiences. Many people from that generation have claimed to have seen the lights prior to the event of 1966. In fact, there are rumors that the lights have actually been seen since the late 1800s by Native Americans. This could refer to the Lac Vieux Desert Band, which settled in the area around 1880. However, there has been no written documentation, and I have not been able to get a tribal band member to respond to my requests for more information.

So exactly what are the ghost lights of Paulding, Michigan? How did they come to be? What legends are behind this unexplainable mystery? To understand the lights is to understand the lore behind the phenomenon. Over several generations, there have been as many stories of the lights as there are theories of what the lights are, but the two main recurring stories are about a railroad brakeman on the job, and the tale of two children playing near the tracks.

More than fifty years ago, the stretch of road now known as Robbins Pond Road lay near an area of railroad tracks. One dark night, fog rolled over the land, as thick as soup. The only creature stirring was a railroad brakeman, who was carrying a lantern to light his way through the thick fog in the darkest part of the night.

All through the night he carried his lantern, swinging it to and fro, walking up and down the tracks as he had done many nights before. Nothing seemed out of the ordinary, but he did not know how different this night would truly be. This would be the night his fate would be sealed.

In the thick of evening, as the brakeman went about his routine, a train had stalled on the tracks. As the brakeman went to investigate, the sound of another train lurked in the distance. The brakeman frantically tried to help get the stalled train moving and out of the way of the oncoming train. Unfortunately, he couldn't get the train to move, and the oncoming train was quickly approaching. The light from the oncoming train was filling the murky darkness like a full moon on a clear night. Sensing the approaching danger, knowing anyone on the other train would be mortally injured if they ended up colliding with the stalled engine, the brakeman bravely fought his way through the thick fog, waving his lantern frantically at the oncoming train to warn the engineer to stop.

As the train got closer and closer, the brakeman waved his lantern as hard as he could, yelling at the top of his lungs, hoping against hope the engineer would hear him or see the glow of his lantern in his path and stop before he collided with the stalled train! The train wasn't stopping! The brakeman moved to get out of the way, but tripped. He tried to get up, however he found the laces of his boots stuck in the tracks. He tried to free himself, but it was stuck. The brakeman tried to loosen the boot to take it off, but his hands were shaking too hard. The light from the train got bigger and bigger until it filled his eyes like a large ball of fire … then he saw no more.

The next day, and for the next fifty years, even today, the brakeman returns every night waving his lantern to and fro to warn others on this stretch of road of the danger of a runaway ghost train. He returns long after the train tracks have gone silent. The brakeman does not return to the site in the flesh, he returns in spirit only. They say the large light in the distance is that of the ghost train's, the runaway train that killed the brakeman, and in fact had hit the stalled train, killing the engineer who now drives the ghost train ever on. The smaller light is believed to be that of the brakeman's lantern, still swinging to and fro, keeping an ever-watchful eye for that runaway train, so that no one else will meet the same fate.

This legend is one of the more famous legends of the Paulding Lights, however, it is not the only legend. There is a similar story, with a few variations.

Many decades ago on a hot and muggy summer night when the air was still, yet thick with fog, two children wandered from home and played near an old military road called Dog Meadow. The children were a young girl and her doting big brother. The trees stood silent as the children ran up and down the train tracks playing tag as they had many times before, with only their small lanterns to light their way.

In the distance, a train was heading toward the children. The children could not hear over the sound of the crickets chirping their song, nor over their own laughter as they chased each other to see who would be "it" as their game of tag continued. They continued playing not knowing the danger was coming ever closer. When they realized the train was almost upon them, they tried to jump over the tracks to get to safety. Only, as they jumped, the tiny shoe of the little girl got caught in the tracks. She fell and broke her ankle. Her brother was not strong enough to carry her off the track. The train was upon them. The brother held his sister's hand as the light of the train filled their eyes. The children died that very night, their lanterns still glowing beside the tracks.

It is said the large light seen in the distance is that of the train, driven ever on by a remorseful engineer who died with grief in his heart, never forgiving himself for the deaths of two children. The smaller lights that still dance are the two children, together forever, playing their games with their lanterns lighting their way in the darkness.

While these legends are the most popular, there are other stories about the lights. Some of the stories include a father who died searching for his missing son and continues his search every night where the lights are seen, a mailman on a dogsled who was murdered on that stretch of road, and a Native American man whose spirit dances on the power lines in front of confused and excited spectators, telling an important story in the lights he creates.

Another final legend about the lights involves UFOs (unidentified flying objects). The first documented case of UFO sightings in the area began a few years before the first documented sighting of the Paulding Lights in 1966. One light watcher told me that she heard the lights were left here by extraterrestrial visitors as a way of collecting information. Information about what? The area, the earth, and about us. The UFO theory is not the most popular theory, but it has gained a lot of momentum among light enthusiasts and believers that we are not alone in the universe. On a side note, UFO sightings in the area have increased in recent years.

No one truly knows what the source of the ghost lights are. The legends and stories are exciting and heart wrenching, but nothing has ever been verified. The one thing I was able to confirm was the existence of train tracks. The Watersmeet Chamber of Commerce stated they were also curious, so they asked a few residents who had lived there all their lives; one an eighty-year-old woman. She verified that the tracks were a narrow gauge railway, so yes; trains did run through that particular area.

Believe It? Or Not?

While studying the phenomenon, I came across many online rumors that the lights once had a bounty of $100,000 by *Ripley's Believe It or Not* for anyone who could prove positively the paranormal nature of the Paulding Lights. The reward was actually more embedded in the legends of the Paulding Lights than even the railroad brakeman.

I did a little digging and could only find contradictory information. Some say it was a rumor, some say it was real but no one was ever able to come up with the proof. With so many different answers, I felt I should go straight to the source. I contacted the archivist at *Ripley's Believe it or Not* who went through past archives. He informed me that he did not find anything even mentioning the Paulding Lights, and didn't think he would. In general, they are always looking for interesting stories to showcase, but they rarely, if ever, offer rewards.

He didn't leave me empty-handed however. He did tell me there was a long-standing competition by the James Randi Educational Foundation (JREF). It is now a $1 million challenge, but in its early years it was $100,000. Armed with this knowledge, I located JREF and was able to ask them about the reward. I hit another roadblock, as I was told they did not offer anything for the Paulding Lights. Their interest was more in proof of psychic and paranormal ability, not paranormal locations. There are many programs similar to JREF that offer rewards for proof of the paranormal, however I was not able to find anyone who would take ownership of offering a reward specifically for the Paulding Lights. At this time, I have decided that this was a false rumor.

Another rumor asserts that the Paulding Lights had been immortalized in an episode of *Unsolved Mysteries*. After making my way through thirteen seasons of the series, I found an episode about another series of lights that occur in Gurdon, Arkansas, known as the Gurdon lights, which is also attributed to spirits who were involved in a railroad accident.

The only series up to this point who have covered the Paulding Lights was a series on the Syfy channel called *Fact or Faked: Paranormal Files*. The series follows a group of experts in various fields who test the most popular cases of hauntings or UFOs to see if they are fact or faked, explainable or still unexplainable. The team consists of Ben Hansen, Bill Murphy, Austin Porter, Lanisha Cole, Jael de Pardo, and Devin Marble along with former team members from season one, Larry Caughlan Jr. and Chi-Lan Lieu. The Paulding Lights were featured in the fifth episode of the first season titled: "Blazing Horizon/Rollover."

The *Fact or Faked* team divided up to investigate two phenomena during this episode. Bill Murphy, Jael de Pardo, and Austin Porter traveled to Paulding, Michigan, and ran a variety of tests to see if they could solve the case of the Paulding Lights. They tried driving a car in the direct line of view turning on and off the headlights, they tested the airplane theory, and did a variety of other tests including an EVP session. By the end of the episode they were unable to disprove the paranormal potential of the Paulding Lights. They left the area perplexed by what they encountered.

What Others Say

The lights have been an attraction for people from all over the country. Even people from different parts of the world have come to witness the phenomenon with interest and bated breath. All are too ready to stare in wide-eyed wonder, and oooh and ahh as the light appears in the horizon, glowing as bright as the moon. Many people are there to see the lights for the second, third, forth, fifth, some for the hundredth time. For a special few, the lights are a tradition, a place for family to gather a few times a year to watch the mysterious lights dance. They return on the same days every year.

When I began my research, I met many of these spectators, the type who are more familiar with the lights than anyone else. Most were more than ready to relate their tales and give their opinions on the light. Some responded to a message board post I placed requesting personal experiences. Here are some of those firsthand eyewitness accounts. Last names have been withheld for privacy. One thing I found out in the course of these interviews is that not everyone simply saw lights glowing off in the far distance. Some saw more that meets the eye.

Megan M.—Michigan—I've been coming to the lights for years now. When I was in high school, my family and friends would camp in this area and spend every night watching the lights, trying to figure out what they could possibly be. Some of my favorite ghost stories were the tales other witnesses would account to us. Spookier than any ghost story you'd get at camp, that's for sure. Some of the stories would send chills up your spine.

What do I think the lights are? I'm going to tell you straight out, I have no idea…but I don't buy the theories out there that skeptics have been throwing around. In my years, I've seen the lights do some strange things that can't really be explained.

I've seen the lights change color, change size… I'm not talking about changing from white to red like most people see. There were a few times I saw the light turn shades of green and blue. There was even an orange and purple once. There was also one time when the lights came a little too close for my comfort.

After my now-husband and I got engaged, my parents, sister, her husband, and my (then) fiancé all came here to see the lights. We were sitting in our folding chairs while my dad was cooking some hamburgers on our portable grill. The lights were happening, as usual in the distance. It was about 11 p.m. and there were maybe three other couples there. We were all just gawking at the light and talking. Suddenly we noticed it seemed to be getting brighter out.

We didn't see anything unusual, so we thought nothing of it and continued with our cook out and conversation, watching the light in the distance. A little later it started getting a bit brighter, but it wasn't a natural moonlit glow; it was more of a reddish glow. We looked at the lights and they were way up in the distance as usual. We couldn't figure it out till one of the couples gasped and pointed up. We looked above us and there was what I could only describe as a reddish-orange ball of light directly overhead. It disappeared the second we looked up.

When I talked about it later with others, they said it was probably swamp gas, or a weather phenomenon or possibly something like a plane passing overhead. Granted, we didn't get a great look, but everyone else saw something too, and it wasn't swamp gas or a plane. How could a plane thousands of miles in the air turn everything all red around us? Not to mention, planes don't just appear, then disappear before your eyes. Two of the other couples that were there with us decided they wanted to leave because they weren't feeling comfortable about staying any longer. That wasn't the first time I've ever seen that happen and even I was a little scared. My dad, a natural-born skeptic, for the first time admitted that there was nothing he could think of that would explain what he saw. He'd pass it off as an optical illusion if we were the only ones who had seen it. I've never seen anything like that happen again.

We waited for almost an hour, but nothing happened after that…and we ended up leaving. We're definitely going to keep coming back to see if that ever happens again. Eventually we'll probably bring our kids the way my parents brought me and my sister.

But yeah, I have no idea what they lights actually are. I just don't think they can be so easily explained away as skeptics try to make them seem. What I saw: if those skeptics had seen it, they wouldn't be skeptics any longer. There is one thing I will mention about that night; I didn't hear any thunder, it was a very clear and cloudless night. I didn't hear any planes or helicopters, no one was standing in front of me with a flashlight going "Ha-ha, fooled you!" No one was in their cars, so there were no car taillights going on and off. What I saw I just can't explain as a hoax or a natural phenomenon. I just don't know. That light was too bright and too close to just be passed off as no big deal. But that's what I saw.

Chris—Milwaukee, WI—I heard about the lights a while back. One of my friends is a former Yooper who told me about them several years ago. He knew all the stories about what the lights are, but I'll tell you, I really didn't buy half of the things he said about them. He said they'd get really close to you, sometimes the lights would fly right over you or your car. He even said people have experienced the lights dancing with them—you move one way...they move with you. I simply explained it all away as illusions from other light sources such as car lights, streetlights, so on. As for the light moving with you, haven't you ever seen those creepy pictures where it seems no matter where you stand, the eyes are looking right at you? I was thinking it's that same kind of illusion.

Out of boredom, looking for something interesting to do, I decided to humor my friend by going camping with him up north near where the lights take place. The first night I was there, by the time we left our campsite and got to where the lights happen, there was a group of people already watching. Everyone was a lot more impressed than I was, I can say that for sure. I was really disappointed as, I swear, they looked exactly like car lights would look from that distance in the darkness.

My friend urged me to take a walk down the path toward the lights. I was more afraid of things like coyotes and bears than I was of anything paranormal, but I took the dare and followed him down the path. With the exception of the light in the distance, it was very dark, and a little too quiet. The further we walked, the darker it got; that is when I noticed something odd was happening.

The closer we got, the further away the lights would look; it was almost as if they were running away from us. I found it a little odd; if they were car lights, the closer we got to where they appeared, the closer they should look and start taking the form of actual car lights. Not only wasn't this happening, I didn't hear the sounds of traffic driving by.

Finally, we got to a certain point where the light all but disappeared from view. I stood there thinking for some time what could make the lights disappear like that. Then it hit me. We came to a point where we were exactly level with the cars, and between us there was some kind of a hill where the terrain got higher, blocking the view of the lights from us. It was the only explanation I could think of. It had to be the trajectory where we were standing.

We walked a little further and I started feeling uncomfortable. Not the "there's a bear in them woods" uncomfortable, just uneasy in a way I can't describe, and I decided it was time to go back. The lights were gone anyway, and there was no telling how much further we'd have to walk to get past the hill hiding the lights from our view. We already walked far enough and now we had to walk all the way back. I'm not much of an outdoorsman to begin with. This was only my second camping trip, and I was already starting to feel the ache in my back. My buddy was disappointed, but he agreed we'd just go forward a little more, then turn back if we didn't see anything still.

About a minute more of walking, we decided we had gone far enough. There were no more signs of the light. He was convinced that we had scared the light away. The legend does say the closer you get, the light disappears. I was convinced we were at the same level as the cars on Highway 45, separated by some kind of a hill blocking the lights from view. I really believed there had to be a rational explanation for the lights.

As we turned around and started heading back, we saw a small red light dash across our path from one side of the woods to the other. My friend freaked out. I have to admit, it startled me, but I theorized it was maybe someone on a bike or a four-wheeler dashing across a path. They have a little red taillight or usually a red reflector on the back. When we came to the point where we thought the light came from, I noticed there was in fact, no path nor road nor trail that any bike, ATV, or car would use, that we could see. We stopped and looked around a bit when a bit of information struck me at just that second—it is dark outside. Bicycle reflectors need light to reflect. It couldn't have been a bike. As for an ATV or car, even if there were a road or a path, ATVs and cars are motorized; you would hear them. Everything was quiet except for a few rustling sounds coming from the woods.

When we got back to the vantage point, a few people asked if we saw anything. We asked if they saw a red light not even a block up the road, and they said they saw nothing except the lights in the distance…the ones that disappeared as we got closer. So the lights weren't visible to us after a certain point, and what we saw wasn't visible to those watching from the vantage point.

To this day I don't have any idea what the heck we saw. I can't explain it away as a bike or car or anything like that. I can't explain why we saw it, but no one else saw it even though it was about the same distance away from them. I have no clue why the lights in the distance disappeared the closer we got. I have no clue, and not from any lack of trying. I've been thinking of everything that could possibly explain what we saw, but I just can't. I don't know if I'm quite at that "paranormal" belief or anything yet…but I'll admit…this is something that has me stumped. It's unexplainable, at least for now.

Mary—Milwaukee, WI—This is my second time viewing the lights. I'm as levelheaded as they come, I just want to put that right out there. I tend to believe everything has an explanation. I don't believe in ghost stories, and I really don't buy into urban legends.

When my husband wanted to come see the lights after reading about them on the internet, I pooh-poohed the idea of it being paranormal right off the bat, but it was pretty compelling from what I read online, so I was willing to see it anyway. My husband and I got a hotel in Ironwood, where we normally stay when we come to the U.P. for skiing, and we traveled to Paulding to see these supposed lights.

When we got there, I was surprised to see how many people were already there waiting to view the lights. I expected it to be filled with people my age or younger (thirties to teens) partying and joking around, but I was a bit surprised to see people there of all ages who took the lights very seriously. Many people were telling us about past experiences about the lights, and their stories were pretty fascinating. They were people like my mother who did not seem to be the type to exaggerate or say things they knew to be untruthful, so I listened to what most of them had to say as we waited for the lights to appear.

The lights began in the distance, slowly at first, then gaining momentum and becoming more frequent, lasting longer each time, getting bigger and closer, then getting smaller and smaller and fading away like someone gently blowing out a candle.

There was one time a bright green light, appearing ahead of a white light, closer than the white light ever came, and lower to the ground. At one point the green light looked so close, you could almost touch it.

One time the light appeared and it seemed to actually lift higher into the sky like the moon rising. It was the strangest thing I've ever seen. It was even more eerie with the sounds of twigs snapping in the woods on either side of us. It was a warmer summer night, but suddenly I started feeling very cold. Everyone said the temperature seemed to drop out of nowhere. Then in the distance, a bright, yellowish light appeared where the smaller white light always appeared. Only it seemed bigger, and flared like it was on fire. It pulsated like a beating heart and changed shapes from a circle to a diamond to an oval, to a blob of light, then disappeared.

Everyone says those are car lights in the distance. What I saw wasn't a car. No way. You'd have to have a bunch of cars to be right on top of each other to make the light that big … and that wouldn't account for the shapeshifting, the pulsating, nor the green light that we saw that night. We're here again trying to see if we will see that same sight again. No luck so far. I firmly believe however, that what we saw that night can't be explained as your average everyday mirage of car lights in the distance, or swamp gasses, or any other natural explanation people have come out with. What we saw is not natural, I'll tell you that.

Kristen—Ottawa, Canada—I'm very familiar with the U.P. We come down here to visit relatives frequently. My grandma lives in Bessemer in fact. So I come to see the lights several times a year and I have for a long time. I don't think I can count how many times I've been here since I was younger. It's been a lot though.

You'll find a lot of us light watchers are repeaters, as they say. It's like we're drawn back to this place by an unseen force. People say there are simple explanations to these lights, but I don't see it. These lights come out every night whether it's a beautiful spring night or a blizzard in the middle of winter. I've been here during a snowstorm, but the light always comes.

I've tried to chase the lights myself, but every time I get close, it seems to run away until it disappears altogether. I've seen it change all sorts of different colors, almost like a Christmas tree with lights of red, blue, green, white, and purple.

There was a time when the lights appeared closer than usual. It appeared almost as if it were halfway up the path rather than way at the very end. There were three lights in a perfect line…a large white one, an equally as large reddish-colored one, and a pale green one. Suddenly, the lights changed and they were no longer in a line. They were in the form of a triangle. Everyone there saw it…and most of us were in awe of it. It stayed in a triangle for about a minute, then one by one they just disappeared.

I never really thought anything of it other than a strange showing from the Paulding Lights, but then someone brought up a weird point. If you notice about 75 percent of the UFO sightings are triangle-shaped objects, or multiple objects that fly in a triangular shape. This isn't the first time the Paulding Lights have appeared to take the form of a triangle.

Many people are quick to dismiss the Paulding Lights away as something simple like car lights. When I described what I had seen when the lights took the shape of a triangle, people would tell me it was most likely an SUV because the back of an SUV has three lights in a pyramid shape. One on top and two where the taillights normally are.

However, they did not see what I saw. Taillights on an SUV are all red, these lights were three different colors. Taillights on an SUV are generally the same size and shape, these lights were not identical in size nor shape. Taillights on an SUV are in a constant shape of a triangle, these lights started out as a straight line, then became a triangle.

Is there a possibility that some of what we see are car lights? Yes, I'll concede that possibly some of the lights in the far off distance are car lights; but the true Paulding Lights do exist. I've seen them on more than one occasion. I've seen them, and I'm convinced there is no natural explanation for them.

Karen B.—Florida—I live in Florida, but I've read a lot of stuff about the Paulding Lights because I LOVE ghost stories. I stumbled on a story of the Paulding Lights a while back, and I have to say, I have been intrigued ever since.

One day I was looking at videos online when I decided to do a video search for the Paulding Lights to see if anyone captured them. I found a few pretty interesting ones. One in particular made me sit up and think. The light on that video seemed so much closer than any of the other videos I've seen. In fact, according to the description, it was taken on a camera with less of a zoom than the video I had watched just minutes before. My husband's camera has a better zoom, and it's a cheap one.

I emailed the person who posted the video and asked what kind of camera they used. It wasn't anything spectacular. So I found it kind of strange. How could a good camera on full zoom get a video of the lights looking so small, yet a camera with a shorter zoom capture the lights bigger and brighter? You think less zoom would mean the lights would seem farther away and smaller. So my interest was once again piqued enough that my husband and I seriously started considering going to Michigan on our next vacation.

Marquette is full of ghost stories, so we thought it would be fun to pack up the kids and take them on an amateur ghost hunting excursion to various haunted places, starting with the Paulding Lights.

My family traveled to Michigan and stayed at a nice hotel. After a good night's sleep, we decided to spend the day near where the Paulding Lights happen. We brought our video camera, a digital camera, and of course our handy EVP recorder. We made sure all of our batteries were fully charged and in perfect working condition. We brought our mini grill and made some hotdogs and hamburgers for the kids while we waited for the supposed lights to start as soon as night fell.

When the sun began to set, I noticed the lights actually started pretty much right away in the distance. They seemed miles away and "moved" fairly quickly. They started off all of a sudden, and after 30 seconds they'd disappear as if they were "driving" away. I was extremely disappointed because right then I knew we were looking at car lights. I wanted to leave because I was so disappointed, but my kids were really excited and I didn't want to tell them what I thought the lights really were. It wasn't fair to break the illusion for them. So we stayed and let them watch.

Maybe an hour or two into the viewing of the lights, my husband nudged me and asked if I wanted to make an excuse to leave. I think he was getting a bit bored too. He must have been thinking the same thing I was. Suddenly my daughter tugged on my arm and said, "Mommy, I think it's coming closer." I looked up, and sure enough, the lights suddenly seemed close, large and bright. It was beating in a way, pulsating. I found that odd simply because the lights I thought were car lights weren't pulsating like that. It also had a large halo around it so that it was shining like the sun. It was nothing like we had been watching for the last hour. This I couldn't really dismiss as car lights.

My husband took out the video camera and started recording, but the camera died out a few seconds after starting. I was upset because I put him in charge of making sure the battery was fully charged. He said he did charge it, but being a typical guy, I knew he probably forgot to plug the other end into the outlet or something. So I took out my digital camera and started snapping pictures at full zoom. None of the pictures were coming out, and after a minute of taking photos, my battery also died. Now, I was in charge of making sure my camera was charged up, and I KNOW I had it on charge, cause the little red light came on when I plugged it in, and it was green when I took it off charge. Perhaps the outlets at the hotel were malfunctioning.

For grins and giggles, we walked down the path a ways to see if we could catch some "EVP" recordings of supposed ghosts that could be "causing the lights." As we walked down the path, the light disappeared, and I turned on my recorder. It too had almost no battery life left. Now that couldn't have been the hotel's fault because the recorder ran on double A batteries, and they were brand new. So the hotel wasn't the cause of our malfunctions.

My other daughter said she could see a green light. When my husband and I looked, we caught a definite green glow before it faded away. I could explain red and white lights easily as car headlights and taillights…but a green light? It was the oddest thing we'd ever seen. Then it was over like that. The lights in the distance appeared again, and that was the last time we ever saw it appear that close, that large, and we never saw the green light again.

We decided to leave since it was way past the kids' bedtime and our youngest (who was only almost 6 at the time) was getting cranky. When we got back to our hotel, we plugged in all of our cameras and charged them till they were full. We tested them out the next day, and they all worked fine. I was able to take a bunch of photos without having to recharge the camera for days after we got home. Same with the video camera. I can't explain why the equipment would malfunction like that for no good reason when they never malfunctioned before and haven't malfunctioned since.

I hear in the paranormal world, it is not uncommon for spirits to suck the battery life out of equipment as they try to gather the power to manifest themselves. I am unsure as to why that happens. It is just something that many professional paranormal investigators say. The only thing I do know, we captured no evidence on the equipment that failed. Maybe there was a spirit that didn't feel like talking that night.

Daniel—Wisconsin—I remember the first time I saw the lights. My friends and I all thought we'd be so cool because were going to show up all those "nuts" who believe in the lights by debunking it. Our main plan was for three of us to stand where the lights are normally viewed behind the barricade, while two others were going to drive to various areas we think the lights were coming from and flash the headlights of the car. We looked around the area for a while to see if there were particular days where the traffic was lighter, so we wouldn't get lost between other cars driving in the area. We wanted to make sure that we could see the lights of our car blinking on and off.

We finally picked a day, and luckily for us, it was light traffic. We got there early in the afternoon and started pretty much right away. We looked over various areas and started driving around flashing our lights. Our friends waited at the barricade said they couldn't see anything. We decided that it was most likely too light outside to get a really good view, so we were going to have to wait until at least dusk.

The traffic was even lighter at dusk, which worked out greatly to our advantage. The reason it was nice was because it meant we'd have a clear opportunity to drive up and down the various roads and have a better chance to see any car lights from where we were standing. I decided to be one of the ones to stay behind at the barricade to see if I could catch the lights of the car, while the others picked which two would do the driving.

Me and two of my other friends waited for the guys who chose to drive to get into place. Once they were ready to drive by, they'd call us from their cell and as soon as they were about to start flashing their lights, they'd let us know. The first time they called, we looked, but we didn't see anything. The lights were obviously not coming from that point. If you drive north a little ways on Highway 45 past Robbins Pond Road, there is another road to the left that goes up a steep(ish) hill. They chose to try the next test from that hill.

Once they were at the right point, they called again and said they were going to start flashing their headlights. Equipped with binoculars, my friends and I watched and waited. That time I thought I may have seen something, but I wasn't 100 percent sure. It looked like a single blinking light in the distance. One of my friends also saw it, while the other didn't.

For me, however, that was an ah-ha moment. Two of us saw something...so we seemed to be onto something. We decided we'd wait till it was darker outside and try the tests again. We theorized that it would be easier to see the lights when it was darker outside.

So when the sun was down completely, three of us stayed behind as before, while the other two drove back to the same location where we thought we had seen the blinking lights. The light was already appearing frequently in the distance, and my friends called to say there was some traffic on the road, and they were holding back till there was some space between them and the current line of traffic. That was another ah-ha moment.

Finally they called and asked if we saw a light. I said no because there was no light at that particular moment. They replied there was a lull in the traffic and they were about to go, so to watch for the blinking lights. They told us they would call as soon as they were into place and ready to blink their lights. So we waited at the ready for that call.

Suddenly we saw a light. It seemed closer and a bit brighter than the other times we had seen it that night. I thought they may be driving with their brights on, so I called and told them we could see the lights of the car, start blinking. My buddy told me it wasn't them yet, as they were just now in position, but they hadn't started. He also told me they did not have their brights on. I told him to start blinking anyway…which he said he did…however the light remained steady. It would pulsate, but not blink on and off.

I asked my friend to verify if there were any other cars on the road, however he told me there was nothing in front of him. He could see a car approaching in the distance, but it wasn't close enough to affect us seeing the lights blinking. I asked how he was blinking them. He stated that he was turning his brights on and off.

My friend suggested that they should actually turn the lights on and off so it would be more obvious. Instead of a bright light and a dimmer light, it would be light then no light. My friend said that he was starting to blink them on and off as we requested, but we only saw the light until it faded away. My friends pulled back up Robbins Pond Road and parked. It seemed odd. Earlier in the day, just before dusk, I was positive we saw my friends blinking the car lights. Or I thought we did. They went to the same spot, and I saw the lights, bigger and brighter than before…but I figured it was an illusion because of the dark, and the use of the brights on the car. However, when they started turning the lights on and off…the light remained, unchanging. They never blinked, they didn't disappear and reappear as they should have with the lights turning on and off…it just didn't make sense.

Did we really see the lights blinking earlier that evening? Maybe we saw the car lights earlier, but these were the real Paulding Lights. Maybe the real light was blocking the view of the car lights…I just didn't know. The only thing I did know…we were unsuccessful debunking this case. We had these big plans, we were going to be big shots…but instead we ended up feeling about 2 inches tall when we had to admit, maybe light believers were onto something…and WE were wrong.

Mary Anne—Detroit, Michigan—I went to the lights with my husband, sister, and her husband. My sister's husband was a true believer of the lights, so he was more excited than anyone else to be going (again). I brought my camera and a digital recorder like most ghost hunting websites said you should be equipped with. I read up on what you should and should not do when doing a paranormal investigation. Prepared myself to figure the lights out once and for all, as I'm sure many before me thought they were going to do.

When we got to the lights, there was this older lady there. She had a camera, a video camera, binoculars, a digital audio recorder, and this thing called a dowsing rod (she called it a divining rod). She told me she was a paranormal investigator who had been investigating paranormal activity as an amateur investigator for almost 10 years, and regularly used all the equipment she brought to an investigation. I asked if she had been to the lights before and she responded with a surprised, "Haven't you?" as if she couldn't believe there are people who haven't been to the lights.

She told me she had been coming for quite a long time. The lights never ceased to amaze her every time she came. As she explained to me and my family about the things she had seen, strange pictures she captured with her camera, strange sounds on her tape recorder, I saw lights off in the distance.

A few other people started pointing and gasping "Oh look! There it is! It's starting." The woman was completely unimpressed with the lights happening in the distance; in fact she rolled her eyes. I was curious about her attitude. She was acting as if the lights were the bees knees when we were talking just a few minutes ago.

"Those aren't the lights," she stated simply. I was taken aback. Those were the lights I had seen in videos online. Those were the lights I had seen in photos—and that was the area maps said the lights would appear. They were the lights, they had to be. "Trust me," she said. "Those really aren't the lights. Everyone thinks they are. I think that's why so many people think they've debunked the Paulding Lights as cars. Because they ARE looking at cars. Its no wonder so many people leave after a short time, disappointed. They see car lights, and leave. They're not patient enough to wait for the real Paulding Lights."

I asked her what the real Paulding Lights actually were in her opinion, since she was so sure those lights were not them, and I turned on my recorder to get her answer. I wanted something I could refer back to in case she said something interesting.

"I have no idea what the lights are. If I did, I'm sure I'd be a rich woman. I'd probably have my own ghost hunting TV show even more popular than those other ghost hunting shows. But really, I have no clue. I just know those lights aren't the Paulding Lights. The true lights come much closer, sometimes they'll even dance with you. No matter where you move, they'll follow you. Many have tried to chase the lights only for the lights to disappear. Many have been chased by the lights as they try to leave the area. I saw the lights myself not even half a mile from where we stand now, it was that close. I'll tell you another thing…the lights aren't as reliable as people think. Those down there always appear come rain or shine, cause there are always cars. However, what I've seen…I went quite a while without seeing what I saw originally. Then I saw the lights almost every night for almost three weeks. It's almost as if the lights can think for themselves. They seem to show up when they want to, to who they want to. Stick around long enough you may see it too. If it feels like it."

After a while I felt a nudge on my arm. The ghost hunter whispered to me and said, "to your left. Look directly through the trees. Follow my finger." She pointed and I looked where her finger was. I saw a greenish light in the middle of two trees in the woods maybe a few hundred feet up the way. I had my husband, sister and brother-in-law look, and they all saw the greenish light, then a small red light. The lights stood there staring at us. The green light was a little higher than the red light, right in the trees. Not on the ground, right up near the top of the trees.

My husband asked me what it was. I shrugged. My sister thought it was maybe an animal and the light of the moon and flashes of cameras from the people taking pictures were catching their eyes and reflecting. But there were so many people taking pictures and talking and making noise, you think most animals would stay away from the area. Plus the lights seemed bigger and somehow more transparent than eyes. I have a cat and I know what their eyes look like in the dark. These were different. I've also had skunks and raccoons in my back yard at night. I see their eyes reflecting when I shine my flashlight to see what's moving about outside. When I turned on the light, they waddle away. Their eyes just look different that what we saw.

I asked the ghost hunter what she thought those lights were and she simply said, "Those are the Paulding Lights. The actual lights." And that was it. She packed up her stuff and said she saw what she came to see. We stayed for at least another hour after those lights disappeared, but we didn't see anything again except the lights continuing in the distance as they had all night long. Eventually we left as well. My brother-in-law is still a staunch believer in the lights. Now I think I am too. At least until someone can disprove what we saw in those woods.

Eric S.—Indiana—I've been to the lights many times. My family would go ever since I was a kid. I went to the lights several times as I got older, and walked north, up the path, towards the lights. The closer I would get, the farther away the lights seemed, until they'd disappear altogether. If you chase the lights, forget it. There's no way you'll be able to catch up to them.

There was one time though that was like, really weird. My dad and I were both walking out to see if we could "catch" the lights, and as usual, once you get to a certain spot, it disappeared. There was no way to get close enough to it. However, this time, something unexpected happened. We turned to head back to where my mom was waiting at the barrier. I had a strange feeling and turned to look over my shoulder. The light was actually behind us. It was a small red light, but it was close. Not even 100 feet away it seemed. I'll tell you what. I jumped so high I could have touched the moon. It was almost as if someone from the shadows jumped out and yelled "Boo."

My dad is a very hard guy to startle…but when he also looked back at nearly the same time, and he saw what I saw. I have to admit, he looked shocked. He even told me he was a bit unsettled by what he saw. He didn't expect it to come so close.

When we got back I asked my mom if she saw anything…but she said she only saw our shadows as we got closer. She hadn't seen any light let alone a red light. My dad and I were pretty perplexed.

I don't know what the lights are. I don't believe it's paranormal or whatnot, but there is something happening out there that is more than simply the reflection of car lights in the distance. I don't know what else to say other than that's my experience … and there's got to be something more out there that we don't know about yet.

Lisa—Minnesota—The first time I went wasn't actually that long ago. I was with three of my friends. There weren't that many people there. I always heard it was pretty packed … but they said it depends on the day and sometimes the month. You'll find more in summer because most high school students and college students are off of school. Naturally there would be more on the weekend than a weekday.

We went on a Wednesday in mid-fall. So naturally it was a bit slower than it normally would be. There were only three other people. It was unusually dark. The moon was out, and there were millions of stars in the sky … normally on a clear night like that, there's a natural light, but I couldn't even see two feet in front of my face. Luckily my cell phone had a flashlight application.

We got to the barrier that stops you from going too far … but nothing was happening. I asked one of the ladies there if they had seen anything, and she said it was out a few times, but she hadn't seen anything in several minutes. Not even a few seconds later, there was a light in the distance. It seemed to be moving, almost like it was falling, and within thirty seconds, it was gone.

A minute later, same thing. Light appeared, started falling, and in less than thirty seconds it was gone. My friend whispered "car." It was obvious that it was a car driving down a hill. I was feeling chilly and I was almost ready to go back to the car to warm up, but something told me to just stay a few more minutes. I was glad I did.

There was a small greenish light under what we thought were car lights. As usual, the white "car" lights seemed to disappear within thirty seconds or less...but the green light was still there. Then it faded out almost like a light bulb burning out, and a red light replaced it. It was almost in the exact same spot. Then there was a white light. Not unlike what we thought were car headlights...but bigger. And this light stayed a lot longer than 30 seconds. It was there for like 2 minutes, then it slowly started to get smaller and smaller, then faded away.

I was thinking about the car theory. I can see how what I saw at first were cars. They would appear out of nowhere, look as if they were falling, (or driving downhill) and in thirty seconds or less they would disappear. They wouldn't fade away. It was boom there they are, then boom there they go. Nothing gradual about it.

The lights I saw later were different colors, and the white light was larger than the other lights, lasted longer, and gradually became smaller and then faded out. For that to be a car, the car would have to be coming towards you, then slowly start backing up. Even if a car did do that, that would not account for how the lights faded away. When lights turn on or off, or come into sight and drive out of sight, it doesn't fade in and out.

I actually started getting a little scared. It was very obvious those weren't car lights. I still think there is something going on out there. I was out there a few more times since that first time, but I haven't seen anything like that again. At least not yet. I plan on going back soon. But there is definitely something going on more than what people think.

Many people had very compelling stories about their Paulding Lights experiences. But what I found most interesting is that these people have never met. They are people from different states, different walks of life, they are different ages, and they have been to the lights at different times. Nonetheless, they all seemed to experience the lights in very similar ways.

Despite how compelling the stories may be, despite how similar their accounts are, there is another side to the story that needs to be heard—the skeptic side. For as long as people have been marveling at the lights, there are those who come to debunk the lights. Many have visited the location, and those who haven't made the trip have studied maps, videos, and eyewitness accounts. From all of that, many feel they have the information they need to claim they have solved the mystery.

Skeptics have many theories that they believe answer the question as to what the Paulding Lights actually are. One of the more popular theories is that the lights are caused by a phenomenon known as will-o'-the-wisps (or simply will-o'-wisps). The phenomenon is also known as corpse candles or jack-o'-lanterns. These are all poetic ways of saying, swamp gas. Swamp gas generally occurs in swampy and/or marshy areas. In these areas, there is a level of organic decay (in most cases vegetation/plant matter) that causes an oxidation of phosphine and methane. The oxidation of phosphine and methane can create a glowing light. Some scientists believe this is what the Paulding Lights actually are.

When the cast of *Fact or Faked* were out at the Paulding Lights for their season-one episode involving the phenomenon, one cast member used a Geiger counter to test for radiation and proved there was nothing radioactive. Another cast member used a combustible gas detector to search the swampy areas for anything that may be releasing gas. They searched the entire area and were not able find any spikes significant enough to have the kind of power needed to create the Paulding Lights. They did not feel swamp gas or radiation were appropriate answers to this perplexing mystery.

Another scientific but more complicated theory is that the phenomenon is caused by what is known as earthquake lights. An earthquake light is a phenomenon that appears in areas of tectonic stress, seismic activity, or active volcanoes. This theory is not as popular because Michigan's seismic activity is relatively small, with the majority of tremors being attributed to man-made events such as mine collapses in the Upper Peninsula. Others are events that actually happen outside of the state. Most recently, an earthquake hit the Quebec/Ontario border in June of 2010, which could be felt in Michigan. That is not to say there is not actual seismic activity in Michigan. There have been documented cases of tremors and quakes in Michigan's history; however, seismic activity in the Upper Peninsula is rare. Earthquake lights are believed to appear as a precursor to earthquakes, during seismic activity, and immediately after an earthquake. Since activity is extremely low in Michigan, it is an unlikely cause; however, it is one explanation many debunkers have considered as a possibility.

The most popular explanation for the lights is optical illusions of cars driving on the northbound and southbound stretch of Highway 45. This theory maintains that people are seeing car headlights and taillights on that stretch of road as it crosses in the direct path of what is now known as Robbins Pond Road. I had a chance to speak to a few of those who believe the lights have natural explanations, one being a gentleman by the name of Philip from Michigan. When I was doing research on the lights, Philip contacted me by email. Here is his unedited explanation:

If you look at the map, find where US-2 in Watersmeet meets Highway 45. Head north for several miles, passed the Lac Vieux Desert Casino, into Paulding, Michigan. There will be a sign that says "Robbins Pond Road" on your right, that's where you turn left onto Robbins Pond Road, which use to be (and on most maps is still marked as) Old US Hwy 45.

If you head up Old US Hwy 45 north for several miles, you will see there is a spot where Old Hwy 45 eventually meets Hwy 45. Now, that itself isn't convincing enough, because once old 45 meets "new" 45, it's a bit out of the line of the viewing area. However, if you go up just a little further north, "new" 45 and old 45 split again.

If you make a left where the road splits, you'll be back in the direct line of the viewing area. Now I remember there being a road, heading out of Paulding toward Bruce Crossing that separates from 45. It is a fairly decent sized hill, and if memory serves me correctly, I believe this is the point on the map where "new" 45 and old 45 split again. That is where I believe the hill is, to the best of my knowledge.

The trajectory of cars going up and coming down the hill will be in the direct line of where people view the lights. Light travels pretty far, and very fast. That could explain why the lights seem so bright at the viewing point. Not to mention someone may be using their brights, and there may be atmospheric conditions that also can play with the appearance of the lights.

I know this explanation won't be good enough for believers…but this is what I believe. If I'm right about the location of the hill I've passed on the way from the lights, then the lights are more likely nothing more than headlights coming down the hill, and taillights going up the hill at the point on the map where the two roads split once again.

Philip's belief was that the lights were merely cars traveling down a stretch of road that intersects many miles up, with Robbins Pond Road. Philip wasn't alone in his belief in the car theory. I spoke to Dave from Wisconsin by email who explained something similar to me about his own theory of the lights.

I went to the Paulding Lights once a few years back. I brought my dad's high-power binoculars with me. They were really strong binoculars he uses when he goes hunting. I went to the area where the lights are seen just before dusk. It was still light enough out, but it's at that time of night where people start turning on their car lights because it's starting to get dark out.

Just as I thought, the light started to appear right at that time, when most people's car lights would start turning on. When I took out my binoculars, I noticed 4 distinct lights. Two side by side, and two more side by side underneath the other two lights. It made kind of an odd-shaped box look. The first set of lights were more than obviously car lights, the second set underneath the first set was an optical illusion of the lights reflecting off whatever surface.

Another thing is that the cars seem to be going down a hill while red lights seem to be going up a hill. There is a hill several miles north towards Bruce Crossing. This could explain why people think the light is moving. Some even claim to see the light rising. It's probably just a car going uphill.

Some people claim seeing the light make a triangle. That's easy enough to explain. When people see that, what they are actually seeing is an SUV. Some SUVs and trucks have two taillights in the normal place where taillights usually are … and there is a third light near the top of the back hatch door, making a pyramid shape. That is what I think people are actually seeing when they think they see a triangle. It's simply a truck or SUV.

I bet if I had something stronger, such as a telescope, I would be able to make out what those lights were attached to, and I guarantee you those shapes would be cars, trucks, and SUVs. Unfortunately I don't have a telescope at this time, but I really believe I saw enough through the binoculars to have come to the right conclusion. The lights are car lights.

I met another couple at the actual Paulding Lights at night. Carly and her boyfriend Justin (both from Michigan) were at the lights trying to figure the lights out themselves. As we struck up a conversation, I found they were less than impressed with the lights; they had come up with a more scientific theory to how the lights were accomplished by cars.

Basically, what I've come to believe is this. I'm not saying this is like, law or nothing…because we haven't really tested the theory…but we've read about this stuff online and it really seems pretty reasonable now that we're here. I'm not a mathematician or geologist or whatever, but I'm pretty good at common sense, and this seems like common sense.

We are on a sort of peak in elevation. If you head past the barricade and keep going a ways, the elevation lowers. According to the internet, there are two hills between us and where the lights occur. The first hill is about level if not a small bit shorter than the elevation on which we're standing at right now. The second hill is about the same level if not a little taller than the elevation we're standing at right now.

So what happens, when you see the cars coming down hill and the light fades out, it's actually at the lowest point hidden behind the hills. Some people say that they see more than one light at times. To me that's just a second car behind the first car. It all makes a lot of sense if you really think about it. I still come out here in hopes I'll find evidence that I'm wrong, but I really don't think so. Everyone on the internet makes a compelling argument in favor of cars. And when I look at the maps and the elevations of the land, I just don't know how it couldn't be.

So as you can see, the car theory is the top theory among many skeptics, and their arguments are very logical and plausible. It had even been put to the test by students at Michigan Tech who used a telescope and were said to not only have re-created the lights with a car, but were also able to discern other lights such as the blue red and white lights of police cars. Their findings did not stop believers, nor did it satisfy skeptics who had theories of their own they believed in more.

One other theory was that the lights were actually created by airplanes taking off and landing at a nearby airfield. While this is not an extremely popular theory, it does have a fair number of supporters. In fact, I heard this theory from a few people when I started researching the lights.

There were a handful of people at the lights the first time I went. Most of them had seen the lights before, but some were out-of-towners seeing them for the first time. I saw one license plate from the state of California. There was one person who had been to the lights before, on more than one occasion, who didn't buy the paranormal explanation, nor the theory that the lights were merely car headlights and taillights glowing in the distance. I asked if she would email me her thoughts for use in my research. This is the email she sent (name withheld per request).

Basically, my husband and I have both come to the conclusion that the best explanation for the lights are
that they are airplanes. There are a few airports in the
general area, so it would not be a stretch to consider
airplanes as a culprit. I'm not sure which airfield they
would be coming from, but I think it's a good possibility. Think about the various things people have
said about the color of the lights and the actions.

First: The lights ascend and descend.

Second: The majority of people see white and
red lights at any given time…but many have
claimed to see green lights.

Third: The white light can be large and quite
bright. Some people say too large and bright to be
car headlights.

I can explain these three things easily.

First: Planes take off, planes land. There is your ascending and descending.

Second: The red, white, and green lights. Also easy to explain. I looked into it and found out about some of the lights on a plane. The navigational lights can be found on either wing of the plane. One wing will have a red light, one wing has a…GREEN…light. On the top of the plane is a rotating beacon, which is also a red light.

Third: The white light that gets large and bright…planes have landing lights that are bright white lights, strong enough to illuminate the landing area as the plane descends.

That clearly explains the various colors of the lights…the red, the green, and the bright, large white lights. It also explains why it seems the lights rise to the sky, and descend. The only thing I cannot explain that has been mentioned by those who don't buy the airplane theory, is the lack of airplane noise in the area. I don't have an answer for that…yet I would surmise that if there were traffic up ahead creating those lights…there should be more traffic noise as well…but I don't hear the constant hum of cars.

Personal Investigation

Compelled by the story of the lights, the various legends and theories, and eyewitness accounts, I felt it was time for me to see the lights for myself. The first thing I did was look into the easiest part of the mystery to solve: the theory that the lights were caused by planes. The best way to decide if this were a viable explanation would be to look at the surrounding airports, air-traffic behavior and compare that information to the location of the lights, and how the lights react.

At the Paulding Lights, the lights people most commonly see are described, by most accounts, as being frequent…appearing all night from dusk until dawn. Some say the light will reappear anywhere from ten seconds to a minute after it fades away.

Now, we are in the Upper Peninsula of Michigan. There are a few airports in the area of the Paulding Lights, but none are major commercial airports like O'Hare in Chicago, or Mitchell in Milwaukee. The smaller airports in the area are used mostly for private planes, charters, and tour planes. Let's take a look at the airports that would be the most likely candidates in the surrounding areas of Paulding, Michigan.

Prickett Grooms Airfield. One mile northeast of Sidnaw, Michigan. It's about a twenty-eight-mile drive northeast from Paulding, Michigan. The airport is actually east of the viewing line for the lights, which places them out of the area of where the lights are seen. However, that is not the main reason this airport cannot be responsible for creating the lights. What rules Prickett Grooms out is that according to the airport's own website, they are not open during winter months, or even when there is snow on the ground. (In the U.P., that can be anywhere from October to even May. Yes, May. I have been in the U.P. when there has been a late April, early May snowstorm.) It is common knowledge that the lights appear come rain or snow or sleet. If the lights are seen in winter when there is snow on the ground…. and we know Prickett Grooms is closed when snow is on the ground, we can rule them out.

Another airport near the area is the **Nikkila Farms Airport** in Mass City, Michigan. It's about a forty-minute drive on US 45 heading north. However, this airport is also east, out of the line of the light viewing area. Also, Nikkila Farms Airport is privately owned/used. Permission from the private owners needs to be obtained ahead of time in order to land on the airfield. A privately owned/used airport is not going to get the kind of air traffic that would cause the appearance of the lights, from dusk till dawn, every sixty seconds, sometimes less.

The next airport worth mentioning is south of the viewing area. **The Northwoods Airport** in Watersmeet, Michigan. According to the website Pilot Outlook, much like Nikkila Farms Airport, Northwoods is privately owned, and permission is required in order to land in the airfield. Again, much like the Nikkila Farms Airport, it would be hard for Northwoods, a privately owned airport, to generate the type of air traffic necessary to cause the effect of the light as frequently as they are said to appear from dusk to dawn.

The remainder of the airports in the general area of the Paulding Lights would be airports such as **King Land O'Lakes** and **Simons Airfield**, which are both in Land O' Lakes, Wisconsin. Based on my research, it is my opinion that these airports are too far removed from the event of the Paulding Lights.

So, for the reasons stated above, I must conclude that the lights cannot be explained as lights from airplanes or airports. So that was one theory I decided was time to set aside. However, to look into the other theories, it was now time to see the lights for myself.

The first thing I did was go online and print out several maps, since I had never been to that part of the Upper Peninsula. As I started looking at the maps side by side, I ran into a bit of a problem. There were several discrepancies regarding the actual location of the lights. I had five maps in front of me—and none seem to agree as to where Robbins Pond Road actually was. Eventually, I asked the Watersmeet Chamber of Commerce for a map. That map didn't help much either, as it also had Robbins Pond Road marked in yet another location.

I spoke to a few people who visited the lights regularly at a restaurant and they gave me simple directions. Go up US–2 until you get to 45, turn left on 45 and continue until you pass the Lac Vieux Desert Casino, eventually on the right side of the road there will be a sign for Robbins Pond Road. When you see that sign, it's an immediate sharp left turn. That sounded much easier than what the maps were trying to claim.

When performing a paranormal investigation, there is one thing I have learned. It is always good rule of thumb to have a partner or team and not go it alone. They may see something you missed, they may hear something you don't hear, and it could boost your evidence if they share the same experiences. And there is always safety in numbers. Safety is very important. So I decided to take my mom, Claire, on this first excursion.

My mom is a very levelheaded person and on top of that she is a skeptic. I knew as a skeptic, she would scrutinize what she was seeing and come up with potential theories that I may not think of on my own. A different perspective to consider; a different opinion to help keep me from jumping to my own without exploring all angles. Plus, as a born Yooper who's never been to the lights herself, she wanted to see it as well.

My mother drove so I could take special notes on the amount of traffic we encountered. I kept a tally of how many cars passed us in either direction, and how many cars were behind us and how many cars were in front of us. I knew this would be important information. During the trip, which took just over an hour and a half, I noted just barely thirty cars. It was a fairly quiet night and traffic was sparse. It seemed everyone was staying in that night.

It was a very cool night, so when we arrived at the place where the lights were viewed on the old dirt trail, I grabbed my sweatshirt as we parked and got out of the car. A few people already gathered at the lights gave us a friendly hello as we walked up to the metal barricade. About half a mile to a mile up there is another barricade. This is due to that stretch of road being constantly damaged by rainstorms and hard winters. It was no longer cost-effective to constantly maintain the area, and thus the barricades. There are no assigned paths, trails, or roads between those barricades.

As I walked up to the area, I already noticed lights in the distance. I was surprised that they were starting before complete darkness. I got out of the car and walked up to the barricade to watch. The lights appeared out of nowhere, and within thirty seconds, appeared to descend and get slightly bigger, then disappeared suddenly. It took quite a while for another light to show up. It seemed like at least three to five minutes had passed. I took out my cell phone and used the stopwatch function to time the lights. When the light did appear, it was the same thing. It appeared suddenly, and within thirty seconds it grew a bit as it made a descent, and disappeared suddenly. And again, after several minutes, another light appeared, this time it looked like two lights…one light in front with another directly behind.

As the first light began to descend, the second light appeared slightly above, making it look almost like the figure eight. In seconds, that light appeared to descend and blended into the first light, then both disappeared suddenly. Five minutes after that, I saw two small red dots, side by side, ascending into the sky and disappearing.

It was becoming obvious what I was seeing. Car lights at the top of a hill, and at a speed of 55 mph or more (even in the U.P., there are leadfoots), it takes about thirty seconds to get to the bottom of the hill. The reason the light appeared to grow a hair before it disappeared was because it was coming toward us—getting closer creates an illusion of looking bigger. And the sudden disappearance could be explained by the car reaching the bottom of the hill below our line of sight, or perhaps by the bend in the road.

The light appeared to be one solid light instead of the two telltale headlights because of an optical illusion due to distance. The same optical illusion that made two lights appear to take the shape of a figure eight, or one solid larger light. Of course, those two red dots were car taillights heading UP the hill, which is why they appeared to ascend. And simply, the lights had such a space between appearances because of the lack of traffic on that particular night. Had there been more traffic, the lights would have appeared seconds rather than minutes after each other.

I have to say, deep down I was kind of expecting it. Everything I had read online had me pretty convinced that I was about to see car lights. I was a little disappointed after being so intrigued by the ghost tales and legends, but it made sense. What I believed to be headlights always started up top and seemed to descend down. What I thought were taillights always started at the bottom and ascended up the hill. Never the other way around; and both types of lights always disappeared suddenly. Regardless, I decided to stay and see what would happen in complete darkness. Would they react the same way?

The night was clearer than I expected. You could almost see every star in the sky. If you looked in the right place, you could even see a satellite quickly making its way across space like a grain of sand among billions of stars. It had been a long time since any of the lights had appeared in the distance. Again, there weren't many people on the road, and the later it got, the sparser the traffic would be. This could account for the fact that the lights were slow to appear, which made the car theory even more likely.

Finally the light began to appear in the distance. Now that it was completely dark, I was able to get a sense for how the light looked when most people saw it. It seemed slightly bigger than usual, mostly due to the light expanding in the darkness, but it wasn't a notable difference in size. Just as before, the light seemed to descend down a hill, although it seemed to take more time than before. My stopwatch clocked it out at 43 seconds before it disappeared suddenly.

Despite a few inconsistencies after dark, the lights seemed to react in much the same way as they did at dusk. Again, I was slightly disappointed, but not completely surprised. I decided to determine when I should tell my mom to wrap things up and head out. I knew it would be a waste of time to watch the lights and expect a different result.

I had heard all of the stories from believers and from skeptics, and now I had seen with my own eyes that those lights had to be car lights. My first instinct was to drop the whole investigation, but I knew I couldn't. I vowed to go through with this, whatever I found. I still had to look at it through the eyes of a telescope and do a paranormal investigation to see if there were any spirits in the area looking to communicate. I couldn't just throw in the towel. However, I was wondering if I should just head home for the night. I wasn't sure what else, if anything, I would actually find considering.

Before I could tell my mom I was thinking of leaving, one of the spectators stated that she felt a little "creeped out." Even my mom, who is not easily unnerved, said she felt chills up her spine. Even I had an odd feeling— almost like there was someone standing right behind me, breathing on my neck. There was no one behind me, but it was such a distinct feeling that I had to look over my shoulder several times to remind myself that no one was there. Just then, a small orange light appeared. It turned a reddish-purple, and then pure red; then it faded out. The second it faded away, a large white light appeared. However, it didn't appear out of nowhere; it started as a small light in the distance and grew. It grew larger and closer than we had seen it all night. it also seemed to ascend upwards toward the sky.

I started timing it a few seconds after it appeared. It did not descend as the lights I was used to seeing did, it lifted higher into the sky, then just sat there, pulsating (another thing the other lights did not do). After two minutes, it seemed to actually grow smaller until it was its original size. It flickered like a candle in the wind, then faded out rather than disappeared abruptly.

I looked at my notes. Two minutes, no descending. In fact it appeared to ascend, larger and closer, pulsating, then growing smaller and fading out rather than abruptly disappearing. It was odd, but I did not have time to contemplate the change in events, for within a few seconds an orange light appeared in the same place. It turned a reddish purple, then pure red again. Then as before, it faded out and a white light took its place. It grew bigger and closer and it sat there. I timed this light pulsating at 1 minute and 37 seconds before it grew smaller, flickered, and faded out like a candle.

Within 30 seconds it happened again. A small multi-colored light followed by a white light that grew, pulsated, stayed just under 2 minutes, grew smaller, flickered and faded away. This was becoming fairly consistent, happening one after another in a short amount of time.

I looked at my notes and started to think. The lights I believed were cars always seemed to start at a point, most likely on top of a hill, and descended down. The light would grow slightly bigger as it drew closer, but then within 30 seconds and 50 seconds, it would abruptly disappear. There were only a few times I saw a red light appear to ascend as if driving up the hill. It was also sporadic, based on the flow of traffic (or lack thereof).

The lights I was witnessing now were nothing like the ones I documented originally. It always started with a small, multicolored light touching the ground, usually between the colors orange, reddish purple, and then red. Then when it faded away, a white light would take its place closer and bigger, growing smaller and then gone. This happened consistently for nearly two hours.

For a car to do this, it would almost have to drive forward, and start backing up. Even if this were the case, when you turn car lights out, they turn off abruptly. They also don't pulsate and flicker, nor to they fade away. Then I began to question the small colored light that always preceded the white light. For that to be taillights of a car it would need to ascend as if traveling up a hill…they did not. Not to mention, they changed colors and they *always* appeared to precede the large white light. Each time you would see this light, you knew a white light would occur immediately after it faded away. It was quite regular.

Cars are not that regular. Some drivers speed, some drive under the speed limit. The faster drivers will pass the slower drivers, sometimes there are three cars heading south and only one car heading north, which means you'd see three white lights and then one red light. Sometimes there are two cars heading north and only one car heading south, which means you would see two red lights and then one white light. If there is more traffic on the road, the light should appear more frequently, if the traffic is sparse it would appear less frequently. Cars and their drivers are NOT this regular.

The small, colored light would appear, and then the white light. In two minutes or just under, it was gone. A few seconds later, the colored light then the white light. Again, too regular. And then there was that strange feeling that overtook the group. An odd rush of nerves that made some people feel "creeped out" *after* this, the "new" set of lights began. This was a curious turn of events.

I took a quick ride from the barricade back to Highway 45. I could still see the lights going off in the distance. Based on the light in my rearview mirror appearing and disappearing, at minimum two cars should be heading south toward me any second. I waited. The only car that passed me was headed north, not south.

And just like that...it was over. Lights were appearing in the distance again, only they seemed smaller, duller, and not as "creepy." I no longer felt as if some unseen person was watching us. You could even see a small red light ascending as if going up a hill. It was time to pack it in and head home. On the ride home, I decided to take note of the amount of traffic on the road again. The cars were still sparse. Traffic had not picked up. In fact, it seemed like there were fewer cars on the road.

When I arrived home, for the next several days I went over my notes with a fine-tooth comb trying to put it all together like a puzzle. I created two columns. The first column described the first set of lights, the second column was for information on the second set of lights. How they looked, how they reacted. After separating them into two columns, I read my notes and started to come to this realization: these two columns may be two separate events.

My mind first wandered to the possibility of a hoax. Could someone be out there intentionally spooking spectators with a flashlight, candle, or possibly even flares? How easy would it be to hoax? How many flares would be needed to create a light that would flare for 2 minutes and fade out and begin again 30 seconds later, and keep that going for hours? I wrote down various possibilities, when my mom spoke her opinions.

"I don't think this could be a hoax."

"Why not?"

"Think of it this way: the first documented case according to your research was in 1966. Some say it has gone on longer than that; however, we know 1966 is the first sighting put to pen and paper. It's now 2010 with 2011 right around the corner."

"Okay, I'm following you so far."

"Think about it. Every night, come rain or shine or snow, heat or cold, wind or calm, dusk till dawn for at minimum, forty-five years. That means someone would have to come out in all types of weather as long as there were people gathering, for forty-five years, to perpetuate a hoax without fail. What kind of personal life would this person have for forty-five years to come without fail to hoax a small group of people? I mean, it could be funny once or twice, but would it really be that funny to them after forty-five years?"

That made sense. Why would someone care enough to come out every day around the same time for forty-five years just to have a laugh? And like she said, how funny would it be after forty-five years? Sunup to sundown, every night no matter the weather, no matter how big or small the group of spectators, no matter if they're just local believers or curious tourists. What would be the point?

Tourism? The U.P. really doesn't need help in tourism. The Upper Peninsula is still No. 1 for skiers, snowboarders, sledders, snowmobile riders, campers, hunters, and fishermen; tourism isn't going to make or break on a mystery light. And who is profiting from a hoax? There is a small gift shop that sells a few shirts and keychains, but it's not so much of gift shop as it is a diner. The diner is called "Strong's," and they seem to sell more burgers than light merchandise. So considering, what would be the point of a hoax for forty-five years at minimum? Not to mention, most who come to the lights usually come for reasons other than the lights. Few have actually come to the area for the lights alone.

I put the idea of a hoax on the back burner. It is always still a possibility, but I've listed it as more unlikely. So I began thinking of an optical illusion. Perhaps in the dark, light travels farther and expands more. This is why it appears brighter and seemed bigger and seemed to last longer in the darkness. However, that really doesn't explain what I had experienced.

At dusk I saw lights I believed to be cars. I noted how big they were, how they were shaped, I even saw how they seemed to descend as if coming downhill, and the red lights I thought were taillights of cars, appeared to head uphill. And they always lasted for less than 50 seconds. In the dark, the lights didn't seem to have changed enough to make note of. They also seemed to continue to head downhill and uphill and last for 30 to 50 seconds...then would disappear as abruptly as they appeared.

The lights that I found to be different from the original lights would always appear after a smaller multicolored light. First the small light would appear, then a white light when the other light disappeared. That white light would grow and either just sit there not moving, or even appear to ascend instead of descend as it should have, and it would just pulsate. Then it would grow smaller and fade out like a candle light rather than disappearing abruptly as if turning a corner or reaching the bottom of a hill. It just didn't seem to fit. Not to mention, these "new" lights seemed to appear too frequently for the amount of traffic on the road. The original lights seemed to follow the flow of traffic with long periods of time between appearances. However these lights appeared within seconds of each other for hours. Was I looking at two different lights?

I had come out of the first investigation with more questions than answers. I was pretty skeptical, and when I noticed a car pattern in the original lights, I wasn't overly surprised. In fact, it was exactly as I expected. However, there was a second set of lights that did not behave in the same way as what I believed to be a car—and those lights had me befuddled, to say the very least.

I decided to take another look at some maps of the area online, once again finding that many have Robbins Pond Road in the wrong place. But when I revisited a map from the Watersmeet Chamber of Commerce, I focused on more of the details. I looked at the area that the lights appeared, I looked for side roads, bike trails, ATV trails, snowmobile trails. Then I decided it was time to head back to the area with more than just my eyes and ears.

Along with my older brother and his wife, I took a video camera and a high-powered Galileo telescope back to the site. I arrived before dusk and began to set up as a few people lingered in the area. One gentleman joked and asked if I was going to "blow the lights up" as he watched me set up the telescope. "That thing looks like a rocket launcher!" We all laughed as I continued to set up. Once I looked into the telescope, it took a little while to get a lock on the location. Using a telescope is quite a different experience. When you look into it, you are actually looking at everything inverted. That is to say, the sky is down and the ground is up. It is upside down, so it isn't easy if you're not used to it.

I finally found my target. I could clearly see the horizon where the event takes place. At the moment, the horizon was empty, so I watched and waited. I pulled out my notebook, again ready to take notes. I had already started making notes on the way up, once again tallying how many cars were on the road on the trip to the lights. There was more traffic than on the first investigation, but it was still surprisingly sparse. Someone pointed out the lights were starting to appear. I looked through the lens of the telescope as my brother started to film the lights on his video camera.

I looked into the telescope and saw two very distinct lights: side by side. There was a set of blurrier lights directly underneath, almost like a mirror reflection of the other lights, most likely caused by an optical illusion of the main lights reflecting off of a surface, such as pavement. I even saw the very distinct shape of a car although the car itself was not in focus. Blurry as it was, it was unmistakably a car. My brother asked to have a look; when he took over, he saw a semi was approaching. Besides seeing the shape of the face of a semi, you could actually see the top line of lights on the hood of the truck, as well as two bright headlights a ways below the line of lights on the top hood. It also appeared to be descending as if driving downhill. You could see the way the truck was sloped that it was traveling down a decline. That meant I was right. There were cars in the distance starting at the top of a hill and descending down.

However, there was still something in the back of my mind. That other set of lights that appeared the first night which didn't fit the behavior of the lights I originally thought were cars. So I decided I should just wait and see what was going to happen. For a while, we saw nothing but cars in the distance.

I didn't say anything out loud about my speculations because I didn't want to disappoint the other spectators who had come to see the lights. I just quietly waited it out. My brother, his wife, and I would just exchange glances as the spectators ooohed and aahed at the lights glowing in the distance, not knowing what we had seen.

It got dark outside; another clear and starry night. The car lights hadn't appeared in quite a while, which was not unexpected considering there was little traffic on the road. When one finally did appear, I looked through the telescope to see if car lights looked different in the dark versus how they looked around dusk. I could still see four lights. They were perfectly round. Two were side by side, with two slightly oval-shaped mirror reflections directly underneath; you could see them moving and descending down the hill. Like the previous investigation, they lasted less than 50 seconds before they were out of sight. Still I waited. As the lights continued, I gave other people that were viewing the lights a chance to look through the telescope.

While others were enjoying a telescopic view, my brother gave a little "huh." Curious I asked what the "huh" was about. He showed me a video he was recording on his camera. It was a Sony Handycam DCR-SX44 with 60x optical zoom.

"I've been recording on full zoom since before dark. Let me rewind a little and show you a few clips. Now, I was pretty much positive what was out there were just cars. Looking through the telescope and seeing the semi confirmed that for me. Now, look at these lights that I'm pretty sure are car lights." He showed me a video of what appeared to be two really small balls of light that looked like a sideways figure eight. The clip only lasted about thirty seconds before the light was gone. He then fast-forwarded the video a short ways.

"Now here is just after dark, of what I believe to be car lights. It is almost the same thing; small white round lights, roughly the same size as the previous clip I showed you. The exception is that, in the dark, it looks more like a single white light than two lights meshed together." I looked at the view screen on the camera and sure enough, there was a white light in the middle of his screen roughly the same size as the previous clip, behaving in the same manner. The light seemed to descend in about 30 seconds and disappear.

"Now that you've seen that, let me fast-forward to the light I just recorded a few seconds ago. It seemed to be, I don't know—just look at this." My brother played the scene for me as his wife looked over my shoulder. The clip lasted 1 minute and 33 seconds…which was 1 minute and 3 seconds longer than the previous, 30-second clips.

"The lights we think are cars are not nearly as long as the light you just recorded. That's kind of what I experienced the first time," I said.

"That's not quite all of it, you're missing the bigger picture, literally. Look at the light, not at the time. The lights we are pretty sure were cars appeared to be a small-sized round or oval ball of light on full zoom. But look at this light; let me pause it here. Right here, this is the light on full zoom; just like the other clips of what we know are car lights." His wife and I peeked at the view screen and had an "aha!" moment.

"That light is so big it doesn't fit on the whole screen when on full zoom," my sister-in-law said. "The other lights looked small and distant on the same zoom; there was a lot of empty space around the lights. This light takes up the entire frame!" I looked closely, and she was right. The top, the bottom, and the sides were actually cut out of the frame. The previous video of what he believed were cars was small and fit perfectly center.

"You'd think that were the oddest part of it." My brother said. "If you look at all the other videos I've recorded since getting here, all the lights are either perfectly round, or oval, or look like two round balls squished together. Look at this; this light is a perfect diamond shape. This is the first clip I've gotten where the light is so big it doesn't fit on the frame, and the light is shaped like a diamond, rather than round in some way."

"Could the size be due to someone driving with their brights on rather than just with their normal lights? The brighter the light, the bigger it would look, right?" I pondered.

"But that much bigger?" my sister-in-law asked. "I mean, double the size, maybe. But even double the size, it would still fit in the frame because the previous lights were so small. That light is like triple the size or more. Comparing the size of the first set of lights he recorded to the size of this light is like comparing grapes to watermelons. This light has to be closer and bigger."

As we discussed the video, I overheard someone talking about the odd way the light was currently showing itself. A gentleman pointed at it and said it was pulsating like a fire in a fireplace. I went back to the telescope and took a peek—and I saw the strangest thing. I saw a light that looked like a ball of fire, and it flickered in the wind. It didn't move, it just sat there, like a flame on a candle. I looked away from the telescope and watched the light with my naked eye. Even without the telescope, it looked oddly pulsating; then it grew smaller and smaller, and faded away.

As one woman took a peek through the telescope, I saw something odd—a small light in the distance, low to the ground. It was glowing, but it was a darker color. The lady looking through the telescope gasped and frantically asked if anyone else saw a dark purple light. It was only there for a second, but I had seen it myself. Someone else admitted to seeing it as well, but it looked green, not purple; where he told me he saw the light was on the other side of where we saw the purple light. Were there two colored lights at the same time in the area? If they were cars, would they be purple and green?

Then, it seemed to be over. It seemed to go back with business as usual. Lights in the distance that appeared to descend, lasted 30 to 50 seconds, and disappeared suddenly. After waiting a while longer, my brother, his wife, and I decided to call it a night. If anything else happened that night, it was after we were gone.

The next time we set out, we decided it was time to do an investigation. Once again I decided it would be a good idea to get to the site before dusk to have enough light to set up our equipment and walk around a bit to see what was going on. When I got there, once again with my brother and his wife, there was an even smaller than usual handful of spectators waiting for the lights to start. I did exactly what I had done before. I started getting set up near the barricade, starting with the telescope. Before I even finish hooking the telescope to its tripod, something happened; something that took all of us by complete surprise. I don't think it was something anyone who witnessed it will forget anytime soon.

A red ball of light calmly glided past in the air, followed by a slightly smaller light lower to the ground than the first; not even 100 feet away from us. Everyone gasped! What had we just seen? Could they be reflectors on the back of a bike. Or maybe an ATV or a dirt bike. No, that's not possible. It was only just barely dusk, so there was plenty of natural light. I could see clear across to the second barricade. I'm 100 percent certain that if I could see clear to the second barrier, I would be able to see a bike or ATV right in front of me not even 100 feet away.

"Here's another problem with the bike theory," my sister-in-law said. "Pedal bikes have reflectors on the back, not lights. Those were glowing balls of lights that cast a glow on the ground. And the problem with motorized bikes or an ATV, even in complete darkness, you would hear the engine revving, considering how close those lights were. And considering the amount of natural light, as you said, we'd have seen a bike or ATV." My brother ventured around the barricade and walked up to where we saw the lights, and looked around the ground.

"No tire tracks or markings of any kind. There is nothing. The dirt is moist here. I can see the footprints I made, so you would definitely be able to see tire tracks."

"And there is one more problem," my sister-in-law added. "Well, more than one. First, there's no path where those lights came from. Where would a biker be coming from and going to in this part of the woods with no path? And wouldn't you hear the crunching of leaves? We're in fall now; half the leaves are on the ground so a bike would make a lot of noise crunching them. Another problem is, look at the side they came from."

"That drop is pretty steep," I stated. On the right side of the road, there was a large hill. On the other side was a deep and thick forest heavy with pine trees. "A bike would have to come down that steep hill only to end up getting stuck in all those trees."

"It wasn't a bike or car or ATV," one of the other spectators stated. "The hill doesn't matter, the trees don't matter, the ground doesn't matter. It's light outside. I can see clear across to the other barricade. If I can see the other barricade, which is at least a half a mile up, we'd see something not 100 feet away from us, don't you think? Those lights were not attached to anything. They were quiet as night, glided gracefully, they weren't even on the same level. One was lower than the other. I can't explain them."

Everyone suddenly said they felt chills up their spine. It made me think of the legend of the children; the large light in the distance was the ghost train, and two small lights were seen that represented the children, the little girl and her big brother who died in the train accident. One of the lights was bigger than the other—perhaps the bigger one was the big brother with his kid sister following close behind? It was strange no matter what. Unless it was a weather phenomenon we haven't yet discovered, I can't explain that by natural means.

One couple left; they didn't feel comfortable staying after what they just saw, especially since they couldn't explain it away. They felt eyes watching them from the woods where the lights disappeared. After a short time, the other couples had departed as well, leaving just my brother, his wife, and myself. I wanted to do a paranormal investigation now that we were alone. I had brought along an audio recorders, a camera, and a K-II meter.

We pulled out the K-II meter and walked around the area looking for high levels of EMF; we waited to see if the meter would spike randomly for any reason. On a K-II meter, there are 5 LED lights. The first green means it's on, the second green means there are little to no man-made EMFs, red is the highest level of man-made EMFs, and in-between there is a yellow and orange light. We waited for several minutes and noticed there were no intermittent spikes at all.

I tested my video camera both on but not recording, and while it was recording. It did not set off the EMF. I tested my smartphone. If I made or received a call or text, it would set the meter off, but as long as it was not in use, it did not cause any EMF spikes. There was nothing else on my person that would cause an EMF spike.

Despite the fact that it was fairly safe to assume I was not going to set the meter off, I still decided it would be a good idea to place the voice recorders at least ten to fifteen feet away from where I placed the meter. We also stood ten to fifteen feet away from the meter and turned our phones off. Knowing I was going to be recording, I made sure to stand as still as possible when asking questions, making sure I didn't move around too much so I wouldn't crush the leaves on the ground. I wanted to make sure I made as little noise as possible. A paranormal investigator I spoke with previously had given me advice about EVP sessions.

"When doing an EVP session, make sure you stand as still as possible. Don't move around too much. Whether indoors or outdoors, you're going to make noise when you move, so try to avoid making too much movement whenever possible. If you must move, make sure you tag it on the recorder. For example: If you are about to sneeze, say 'This is me sneezing' before the sneeze or 'that was me sneezing' after the sneeze.

"If you have to walk forward, state on the recording 'You will now hear footsteps as I walk.' Then announce when you have stopped walking. Even if you burp make sure you say 'that was me belching.' If you don't tag each sound, it will be hard to remember after the fact the noises you make, and you may mistakenly take a sigh you heaved as paranormal. That will throw off the entire integrity of any potential real EVP you may catch."

I made sure to adhere to that tip. As I walked away from the recorders, I made sure to announce it so that when I heard the footsteps, I would know it was me. Once I was in position, it was time to begin.

I began by announcing myself and my brother did so as well. Then I explained my intentions to any potential spirit that may reside in the area. I let any spirit know that if they existed and if they were curious about us, to not be afraid. We were not there to harm them nor to tell them to leave. We just wanted to speak with them and get confirmation of their existence.

I took a second to explain the K-II meter. I explained if they wanted to let us know they were there, they'd simply have to stand next to the "gray box," touch it, walk past it, and it would make the lights on the box blink. I let them know that we tested the area and that it has sat there all this time and has not lit up once. So if these lights light up as strong as possible to our questions, we may know they are around.

This was the big investigation. This was the investigation where I was finally going to find something, or come out empty-handed—the investigation that was going to make or break the Paulding Lights. I wanted to make sure I did everything right so as to not hurt the integrity of whatever I may catch on the recorders.

I had a strange feeling that night. A creepy feeling that made me not want to be there. It was like I was being watched from the woods by a pair of unseen eyes. Despite the fact it was warmer than a usual fall evening, I felt an unusual chill right down to my bones. It was an odd sensation. However, I stood my ground and began the EVP session. I asked all the basic questions.

"Is there anyone here with us?" I stopped to give time for whatever may be with us to answer. "If you're here with us, you need to do something to catch our attention. We want to know you're here. There are two black boxes. Speak loudly and we will hear you. Or you can walk by this gray box (the K-II). Touch it, stand by it, and it will light up to let us know you're here." I paused again to give the spirit a chance to answer.

The odd thing was that I was feeling out of sorts. I was still feeling watched, I was nervous, and I had a hard time concentrating. I had all the questions that I wanted to ask in my mind, but for some reason when it was time to start to asking those questions, I just couldn't seem to remember. Ever since those red lights floated by, it was all I could think of. So there would be awkward silences. My sister-in-law had gone back to the car by the time we had started the EVP session. She was feeling a bit uncomfortable. I whispered to my brother, quietly asking if she was okay, and my brother whispered back that she said she was fine, she just wanted to go back to the car. After a few minutes of quiet, my brother took over asking a few questions.

"People say you don't exist," he began, trying a different tactic than simply asking questions. "They say there is no one in this area. They say that the lights in the distance are merely cars. Must kind of stink to hear that people deny your existence. There must be a reason you manifest yourself almost every night for so long. You must want people to acknowledge you. So if you want to be known, that's why we're here. Manifest yourself in some way to let people know you do exist. You just have to manifest somehow." My brother paused, (sniffed once) then paused again.

After about a half an hour after I started the investigation, people began to gather at the lights again. I knew it was time to pack it in for a while. One car wouldn't be a big deal. If we explained what we were trying to do I'm sure I could have gotten them to cooperate so we could continue our investigation. But two cars of people, then eventually three, was beyond my ability to control the investigation, and continuing would compromise the work we had already put into that evening's investigation.

As it was, I was already off my game. I couldn't shake the feeling that I was being watched. I felt unnerved. So the interruption of new light viewers was a welcome sight, giving me a reason to call it a night. The moment I got home I uploaded the sounds to my computer, went into a quiet room, put on my headphones and started listening. I wasn't sure I would find anything since the investigation was cut short.

There wasn't much going on in the beginning of the recordings. Things seemed fairly slow. I was starting to wonder if we had caught anything at all. The only thing I heard was my voice, and the voice of my brother and sister-in-law. I heard us speaking a few times, tagging a few sounds, "This is me walking away," or "This was me coughing." The recordings seemed fairly mundane.

Then I came to the audio of myself saying that if there was a spirit with us, it would need to make itself known. It would need to do something, anything to catch our attention. Then I explained what the boxes were for and how they could speak into them so we could hear their voice or make the K-II meter light up. After a short pause, I heard something that got my attention. I heard what sounded like a soft whisper of "Hey"…then there was a slightly louder whisper, "HEY."

It sounded male, and it sounded as if it had been said directly into the microphone of the recorder. It was as clear as if there had been an actual person standing by the recorders. Since the recorders were in my sight at all times, I knew that was not possible. My voice and the voice of my brother sounded very quiet and in the distance compared to this voice. It was so clear. The very sound sent a chill up my spine. It was so clear, so distinct, almost as if someone had been standing right there. No matter how often I hear an EVP, it always feels a little unnerving to hear a voice belonging to someone you can't see. They're there, but you just don't know it.

Whenever I whispered to my brother, or moved, or burped, or even sneezed, I would say "This is me or him doing such and such." So I knew it wasn't either of us saying "Hey." Again, we were standing a good distance away from the recorders, and you could hear that by how far our voices sounded. It just wasn't us. The only other person there besides me and my brother was his wife, and the voice was definitely male. I isolated the sound, and then continued to listen through the entire audio. I was hoping I'd catch more than just that.

I came to the point where my brother and I were whispering to each other. We were so quiet, had I not known what we were talking about, there would have been no way to hear our conversation. As we whispered, I heard a loud sound, very loud; it was like the sound of someone saying "Eh," almost as if it were annoyed that we were talking amongst ourselves and not to it. It was just an utterance, but it was clearly a voice. It also sounded like a male voice, but it had an odd tone to it. I isolated the sound to save for further review later.

The one that really got me most came when my brother was speaking to the spirit. Instead of asking a direct question, my brother was talking to the spirit—treating the spirit as if it could still be a living entity. Having a conversation that any two normal people would have. He explained that people didn't believe he existed, yet we knew he wanted to be known, so he needed to manifest for us in some way. There was a pause, then my brother sniffled, and during the pause that followed, I heard what sounded like a hearty chuckle, followed by "Okay"; the same voice that sounded like it was saying "Hey."

This was a definite male voice, the "Okay" was as clear as a bell, and I knew it was not my brother's voice. Also, once again, it sounded right into the microphone. The laughter also got me. It was almost as if whatever else was there with us, found us and all our silly questions amusing. It was also not a random response. My brother asked for whatever was there with us to do something to prove their existence, and the answer was, "Okay."

There were several other sounds I had caught. Some that sounded like words, others that sounded like laughter. One in particular sounded like a voice asking a question of us, "Who are you really?" followed by what sounded like a chuckle. There was a part when I heard "I'm here" immediately after a question of "Is anyone with us now?" When I could be heard snapping pictures on my camera, I heard what sounded like a male voice saying "Stop!" as if to say he didn't want his photo taken. There were many other EVPs. When asked to say something or make the K-II light up I heard "I'll try." There was even a time when what sounded like Native American chanting was heard faintly as we asked if whatever was there was native to the land.

However, many of these sounds were compromised. They happened when we were moving, or when someone coughed, or by the wind. They were not as crisp and clear as these particular sounds that I isolated. I knew I caught more, but these were the clips that were not compromised in any way. So I set the rest aside as personal experiences, and classified these clips as evidence.

I contacted an EVP expert from a paranormal society that a friend recommended to see if that person could help me with the clips I believe I had captured. If I captured anything, I knew this person would be the one to tell me.

The investigator emailed me right after listening to the clips. She said she could hear what I had heard, and there were a few other things she heard as well that I had missed, in the background—things that take experience to hear. Another investigator who offered to listen to our audios came to the same conclusion. The only thing he could not say for sure was the "Eh" sound. He said it could be "Eh" or it could be a "Heh" but it could also have been a natural sound that slipped by us. He couldn't be sure. It was unclear. However he stated the rest was clear in his opinion. I had caught some good EVPs.

A nice person from the paranormal message board emailed me and asked if I could send him the audio clips so he could clean them up and have a better listen. After a while, he emailed back his findings. He stated that if I was tagging all the natural sounds that occurred as I said I had, leaving little doubt as to what was merely us moving or talking or sneezing or coughing; then he felt there may be something to the audios we captured. He agreed with the previous investigator. The "Eh" was too iffy. While it sounds like a voice, there could be a natural explanation too; however with the laugh followed by "Okay" and the "Hey, HEY," there was something to those EVPs. However, he did not hear "Hey"…"HEY"…as I had heard. He believes he heard "Help"…"HELP," something I found interesting.

I was fairly convinced. I had caught something I couldn't explain: a male voice that could be heard clearly. And I believed I caught other audio clips of the male voice as well, just not as clearly as these; but they were there. However, these clips were clear. In these clips, no wind was distorting the sound, and the sound wasn't in the distance, it was right into the microphones. In some cases, they appeared on one recorder and not the other. Also, because I was careful to tag all of the sounds that were caused by myself or some external natural force, I knew these sounds were sounds neither I, nor my brother, nor his wife caused.

Then there was the unsettled feeling I had, which was more unsettled than in previous investigations. It was like someone else was there watching us, unseen. And what about the phantom lights? Just a few feet away, still light enough to see they were not attached to anything, floating silently along their way. Those lights would not be the last I've seen at the site. Shortly after these events, on another night of investigations with my brother and his wife, a green round ball of light hovered momentarily near the barricade just a few feet away from where I stood as I was packing up to leave for the night. It cast a glow on the fresh snow that had fallen, and reflected in the metal barricade. I blinked in amazement, and it was gone.

I gathered all of my notes and evidence on the Paulding Lights and reviewed them. Many who have seen the lights agree that there are lights that are multiple colors including red, green, yellow, white, and sometimes purple and orange. As I stated, I myself saw the two red orbs and a green ball of light. I was not the only witness to these lights. My brother, my sister-in-law, and other spectators also saw these lights and could not explain them.

Many have stated that they have seen lights that are more interactive than the lights in the distance. Lights that come closer to where you stand, lights that follow you or disappear when you chase them. That coincided with my experience. The lights I saw were not in the distance, they were just feet away, close enough you would think you could touch them.

When looking through a high-power telescope I did see the shapes of cars; my brother saw what he knew was a semi-truck. I saw the car lights descending down apparently as if going downhill. I saw taillights ascending almost as if going up a hill. I saw the outlines of vehicles that left no doubt they were car lights. Most of them descended/ascended that span of road in the general time it would take a car going 55 to 60 mph to drive. It was very easy to conclude without a doubt that the lights in the far distance are car lights. The lights would grow bigger in the complete darkness, then disappear suddenly as it disappeared from the direct line of view. The pattern was that many of the lights we believed to be cars lasted anywhere from 30 to 50 seconds before disappearing.

Then there were lights that seemed larger, closer, and appeared longer than what we know to be car lights. They flickered and pulsated, grew bigger and then grew smaller and faded out rather than disappearing suddenly as the car lights had done. It was almost always preceeded by a small multicolored light. They did not follow the same pattern of the lights we knew to be cars. These lights also seemed to last longer than the lights we knew to be car lights. Some lasted anywhere from 1 to 2 minutes. I took stills of the video my brother had taken of what we knew were cars, and an unidentified light and put them side by side. The car lights at full zoom were small and distant looking; they also looked like car lights. Two round lights meshed a little together to form a sideways 8. The unidentified light at full zoom was so large it didn't fit the screen, and it was a single light that was shaped like a diamond.

Back to the two red lights dashed out not even 100 feet from where we stood. In that particular area, there is a hill with a sharp drop on one side, and a thick gathering of trees on the other. For any bike or motorized vehicle to have been in that area, they'd have to have dropped off that hill and been able to make it through a tight clench of pine trees. My brother looked at the path where the lights glided. Nothing had been disturbed even though the ground was moist enough for him to leave noticeable footprints as he walked. There were no tire tracks or fresh footprints besides my brother's. No one heard motors, and we did not see bikes or vehicles. These were lights that seemed completely unattached to anything, and everyone there at the time witnessed them.

During an actual EVP session using digital audio recorders and external microphones placed in controlled areas, I was able to capture a few distinct, clear voices.

"Hey…HEY." (or Help…HELP as someone else heard.)

"(laugh) Okay."

"Eh" or "heh."

There were several other captures, such as a voice that sounded as if it were saying "I'm here," "Stop," and "Who are you?" However those were the ones that were compromised in some way, either by us speaking, moving, or the wind. One thing I can say, no matter what EVP we captured, whether it was the laugh and "Okay" or "I'll try," it was always a male voice and was always seemingly in response to questions. If asked to do something to make themselves known, we heard "Okay." When taking photos, I heard "Stop" as if to say, "Stop taking photos." It wasn't like I was asking "What is one plus one?" and got the answer "Bojangles." Each EVP I seemingly caught seemed to be a logical direct response to a question.

I looked at all of these things that we had collected during the several investigations. I looked at my back research. I looked at the stories of others who believed in the lights. I looked at all of the different angles of those who did not believe in the lights. I looked at all of the scientific explanations as to what they lights were, then I looked at my personal experiences. Especially the times I felt unnerved, like something more was there, watching from the woods.

For hours I sat looking at that journal. I went back and listened to all the audio and then watched all the video all over again. When I was finished, I went back yet again and read all of the journal entries, listened to all of the audio, and watched all of the video yet again, and again, and again. I made sure that I was careful to not miss anything. I didn't want to miss any sounds or anything that may have appeared in the video. I wanted to re-read everything I wrote down in my notes to make sure I left no stone unturned. I even returned to the site and did subsequent investigations.

Then I poured over the evidence presented by multiple debunkers that have concluded the lights are car lights in the distance. I read all of the trajectories, all of the angles, all of the experiments. I read articles on swamp gas and conditions necessary for swamp gas. I read about how light travels, how light expands and retracts, and how light may bend if reflecting off another surface. I researched the airports in the area. I checked all of these reports and documents against my journal entries.

I had seen cars through a high-powered telescope. I had taken video of two distinct headlights and had seen the way they drove down as if heading down a hill as well as the way taillights headed up as if driving up a hill. I saw the shape of cars, SUVs, I even saw the shape and distinct lights of a semi. I had driven past a hill as I headed north on 45 that would be a possible culprit for the incline and decline that would cause cars to ascend and descend.

Then I wrote back those who had emailed me their stories to ask them to re-explain what they had previously told me. I wanted to see if there were any discrepancies.

In the end, their stories were the same and their feelings about the Paulding Lights were unwavering.

I looked back at the information and advice a few paranormal research groups had shared with me. I looked back at our various email conversations about the Paulding Lights and reexamined their opinions both on the original video and audios I sent, and on the new evidence I sent.

Finally I took a look at all of the Paulding Light legends: the children killed by an on coming train, a railroad brakeman killed by a train, and a Native American man dancing on the power lines and telling his story. I looked at all the similarities and differences between the various stories and legends on the Paulding Lights.

I looked over everything I possibly could for the next week, devoting hours a day to putting all the pieces of the puzzle together. Finally, I believed I had my answer. I have found beyond a doubt in my own mind that the Paulding Lights DO exist. It is not always what people believe it is. Many people see what I believe are cars and jump to the wrong conclusion; however, the hauntings in the area are very real. I firmly believe something is in those woods on that old stretch of military road that defies explanation.

I do not think there will be anything from any side that will fully convince anyone that the lights exist, or that they don't. That is what makes these lights even more mysterious. If I captured a phantom voice saying "I am the cause of the lights" and played it for skeptics, they'd say that was nothing more than the wind making it sound like someone saying "I am the cause of the lights." Yet if a skeptic shows a believer all the reasons the lights are nothing more than car lights in the distance, the believers will simply shake their heads, unwavering in their belief, sure of their own experiences. Something still draws people to this area, skeptics and believers alike.

What are those lights you see in the distance? Are they cars? Or are they the Paulding Lights? What is that noise in the woods? What was that whisper in your ear? Is there a ghost that still haunts these woods? Perhaps there is a brakeman warning of a runaway train. Perhaps there are still children playing their games of tag while a remorseful engineer drives the ghost train ever on. Perhaps there are many spirits in the area, a collection of energy creating the bright lights that dance with spectators in the night.

There also could be a natural explanation for the lights. Maybe they are swamp gases being released from within the earth. Maybe there is a natural phenomenon we do not yet know about to blame for the lights. Perhaps the lights are not ghosts after all. Maybe the actual ghosts that forever wander the earth are standing **right by your side**…watching the lights with you.

four

The Rocking Chair

....

Object attachment can occur when a spirit wishes to hold onto an object. Whether it was an object beloved to them, or one they come across that reminds them of their mortal life, they will cling to that object and follow it where it goes, trying to hold onto that piece of humanity.

Many people, no matter where they live, have been struggling with the paranormal on their own for decades. Most are too afraid of ridicule to seek help. Thanks to the growing interest in the paranormal and shows that make ghost hunting mainstream, they're finally speaking up. One such family turned to me for help figuring out what had been happening in their home. Were they going crazy, or were they dealing with something paranormal?

With permission to tell their story, due to the sensitivity of the material, they asked to remain anonymous, so their names have been changed. I will call them the "Roberts." Tom, Mary, and little Bernadette.

The Roberts were a very friendly family. They had been married for five years, and had a two-year-old named Bernadette and another one on the way. They had lived in the Upper Peninsula of Michigan all their lives. They met at college. They laughed when they found they had practically been neighbors growing up, they even went to the same high school, but never knew it. The backdrop of their engagement was a beautiful waterfall one late spring day in the Upper Peninsula, and they planned on raising their family here as well.

Mary gave birth to Bernadette at a hospital in the great northern woods, proud to have brought another Yooper into the world. They settled in to their quiet life with their little daughter in a small but cozy house. This happy little family enjoyed life for close to two years until Mary and Tom realized they were to become parents again—and the happy little family was about to get a bit bigger. Now, with a new baby on the way, they realized they were outgrowing their small home and needed to upgrade to a house with one extra room. Their current home had a tiny yard, and they also wanted more property. The only other requirement was that the new home be in the Upper Peninsula they loved so much. Tom and Mary started searching for a property before their house was even up for sale, but nothing was striking them as what they needed.

After having their home on the market for two weeks, it already had interested buyers. The push was on to find the perfect house while they were waiting to hear if the buyers were approved for financing. If they were and the deal went through, they would have no place to go without a house of their own to put a bid on. It seemed as if they were never going to find a place that met their needs, until, there it was.

The home with three bedrooms and two full baths was in a quiet part of the Upper Peninsula on about three acres of property. It was a nice little area surrounded by trees, with neighbors on either side. They liked that it was private, but not secluded. The road was a quietly traveled road, which was a nice change from the main thoroughfare they were currently living near. All night long, they could hear traffic buzzing by. Sometimes, late at night, a semi would blare its horn at an inconsiderate driver and wake up little Bernadette. A quiet road would be a good change of pace.

The house was an older structure, but seemed to be well maintained by the previous family. The cabinets were all new and made of oak, which matched the hardwood floors that had been installed the previous year. The roof had been repaired five years earlier and was still under warranty, and the electricity had been upgraded to bring it up to code. Most of the main work was already done, so the house was move-in ready.

It was perfect. It had the extra bedroom they wanted for the new baby; it even had an extra bath. It was on a quiet road, and it had the yard that was large enough to set up a playground area for Bernadette. A slide and swing, maybe a trampoline for when she got older. There was also a nice patio in back for the hot tub they always wanted, and with the reasonable price, they would be able to afford it all. They didn't even need a second showing—this was the house they wanted, and they were ready to sign the papers.

When they moved in to their new property, they were extremely happy. They had gotten the house for nearly $10,000 under the asking price and sold their old property for just about what they had asked. In the end, they came out with a small profit, which they used to buy the playground set for their daughter, and the hot tub for themselves. They replaced the rose-colored carpeting in the living room with a nice neutral cream-colored carpet, which provided a striking contrast against the red and brown brick, wood-burning fireplace. However, Mary felt like something was amiss in the living room.

After arranging and rearranging the furniture, they realized their couch, love seat, and recliner were too big and bulky for the sophisticated space. They bought new furniture: a sleek brown couch, a chocolate-colored leather chair with matching ottoman, and a chocolate-colored leather rocking recliner. Although the new furniture fit the sophisticated feel of the room, they felt like something was still missing. That's when Tom realized they were short one seat. Before they had a love seat, which sat two. Instead of a love seat, they opted for a chair. It seemed to Tom and Mary, there was an empty space that needed one more piece of furniture. They just didn't know what would go with what they had.

For a while, they kept the room as it was. The new furniture didn't take up nearly as much space, which left room for baby Bernadette to play. One day, not long after moving in, Mary's parents came from Wisconsin for a visit bearing a special gift.

"It was a beautiful antique rosewood rocking chair. She found it at an estate sale," Mary stated. "It was an interesting piece. The details on the back were very intricate. My parents didn't know much about it, only that it was originally handcrafted fifty years earlier as a gift from the first owner to his wife for their anniversary. I placed it near the fireplace and was immediately in love with it. It was just so romantic looking. I could imagine myself sitting on the rocking chair with Bernadette, reading her a story, rocking the new baby to sleep. I even pictured myself placing my rose-colored crocheted afghan on my lap and snuggling next to the fire with a good book on a cold winter night. It was exactly what we had been missing. It made up for the seat we lost when we chose a chair over a love seat."

The thrill of the new gift wore off rather quickly. Within a week of the rocker being introduced to the house, odd things started to happen. The first thing the Roberts noticed was Bernadette acting strangely. She kept talking to the rocking chair in her tiny little baby-girl voice. She was having a full conversation with the chair as if something was sitting on it. She had never shown interest in make-believe friends before. At two years, eight months old, they thought she was too young to have that kind of imagination. When asked who she was talking to, Bernadette would only point and say "the man." They weren't overly concerned until this became a regular occurrence, usually around the same time at night. Eventually, worried that something may have been wrong with her health or development, they went to her pediatrician.

The pediatrician was less concerned. He stated most children have imaginary friends starting at the age of three, and she was just four months shy. She was developmentally normal for her age. She was starting to count and say the ABCs, and she knew how to use certain words in ways that wasn't merely mimicking. When she said "I" or "me," she knew it was in reference to herself and something she wanted or did or said. She knew how to ask for what she wanted. Of course, she also babbled at times and it was hard to understand her when she began talking a million miles an hour, but that was also normal. Everything was normal, but it wasn't. Bernadette kept talking to the rocking chair and would only say "the man" when asked. They chalked it up to an imaginary friend. As the pediatrician stated, around age three is when imaginary friends first start to emerge. But why a man? Most little girls dream up talking ponies or fairy princesses; who was "the man?"

One night, Bernadette was staying at Tom's parents' house. They had started taking Bernadette for overnight visits as Mary's due date approached, in case they had to rush to the hospital in the middle of the night. She was due any day. Mary couldn't sleep as she was having a case of acid reflux, something she frequently had during her pregnancy. She got a small glass of ginger ale and a book, and sat on the couch with a blanket wrapped around her. She was a few chapters in when she thought she saw something move out of the corner of her eye. Did Tom just walk by? She looked around but didn't see anyone. She listened carefully and could still hear his snores coming from the bedroom. She passed it off as nothing and continued reading.

Suddenly, Mary heard a squeaking sound. She looked around and noticed the rocking chair was rocking. She got up and walked over to it. She felt how cold it was around the chair. Maybe there was a pocket of air that came through the fireplace and caused the chair to start rocking? It would have to be a strong pocket because the room was carpeted. Rocking chairs don't normally rock on carpeted floors from a small breath of air. She walked over to the fireplace, but even the brick was warm. There was no air coming in.

She didn't think much of it and simply moved the rocking chair away from the fireplace. She went back to the couch and started reading again. After a few minutes, she heard was the same squeaking sound. She looked up—the rocking chair was rocking again! She moved the chair again and went back to sit down and watched it. It was completely still. After a few minutes it started rocking again. Now she was getting scared. Rocking chairs just don't rock like that on carpet unless someone is sitting in it, rocking. Frightened, all she could do was say "Stop it," and the rocking ceased. She ran into the bedroom crying to her husband.

Ever since, the chair rocked on its own no matter where it was, and Bernadette always talked to the chair in the evening as if there was someone in the chair. They didn't know what to do. It was one thing for the daughter to have an imaginary friend, but what about Mary? Tom was seeing the chair move on its own as well. Like Mary, he moved the chair from place to place, but it always seemed to start rocking.

A few days after Mary first noticed the chair rocking by itself, they welcomed baby Daniel into their family. Things seemed quiet for a while. Then, one night, Daniel got up crying. It wasn't unusual. It was around the time of night he needed a change or feeding. Since he had already been fed, it must have been potty time. So Mary woke Tom up to take his turn getting the baby back to sleep. As Tom wiped the sleep from his eyes, the baby stopped crying. Did he go back to sleep? Tom got up and went to check in on the baby just in case.

Tom quietly peeked into the nursery. He saw the mobile above the crib swaying back and forth. It was unusual. The mobile spun around and played music when it was on—but the mobile wasn't on. It looked as if someone was tugging on it to make it move. The baby was calm and just cooed in the crib with big, wide eyes staring up at the mobile. Tom picked the baby up and felt the diaper. It was wet. As he changed Daniel, he wondered what would have made Daniel stop crying. Normally when Daniel had a wet diaper, he would cry before and during the changing, and calm down once he was dry and being cuddled. He also couldn't explain why the mobile was moving. It felt like someone was in the room. That is when they felt it was time to do something. That is how I came to meet the family.

One of their friends was into paranormal investigations. I had met her and her husband at the Paulding Lights when my mother and I first went to investigate the phenomenon. We had stayed in touch via email, when they wrote to me and asked if I would like to tag along to see the house. I agreed and met them at the residence one late afternoon. The Roberts told me the whole story before heading out to Tom's parents' house to sleep for the evening, leaving the house empty for the investigation. The husband and wife team and I quickly began setting up the equipment. I had my K-II and audio recorders. They introduced me to the Mel meter; the first time I had encountered the equipment. Shortly after, I purchased one for myself. A Mel meter is an interesting paranormal investigative tool; it is one of the few pieces of equipment created by an investigator specifically for the purpose of paranormal research. It reads electromagnetic fields as well as fluctuations in temperature. It alerts you when there is a major change in either.

Much like we believe a spirit can manipulate EMF to communicate, it is also believed when a spirit is nearby, it draws in energy to move objects, to speak whether audibly or to be heard via recording, and to move about. This can cause sensations of wandering cold spots. A Mel meter can detect a sudden drop in temperature that could indicate a spirit is trying to manifest.

Once we were set up for the night, we divided up. I stayed in the living room with my recorders and the rocking chair. The couple covered the nursery and the little girl's room. No activity was found in Bernadette's room, but we felt it was a good idea to do an investigation since Bernadette seemed to frequently speak to "the man."

I started my own investigation by waiting and not speaking. I just looked at the rocking chair and waited for it to rock on its own. I walked around and touched the walls, the fireplace, and the walls inside the fireplace. I walked by the windows. I couldn't feel any drafts or pockets of air anywhere. The walls felt normal for the temperature inside the house. The chair did nothing.

I looked for the vents where the heat and central air would come through. I found the thermometer and turned it up a bit to get the air to kick on, after making sure the other two knew what I was about to do. I heard the air whirring, I felt the registers and air was coming through strong and cold, still the chair did not move. I turned the air off and investigated the chair itself. I pulled it back, and let go. It rocked once and then stopped. The soft carpeting prevented the chair from getting enough momentum to rock back and forth as it would on a hard surface. I could not explain what the owners had experienced based on what they described. I could not get it to reenact using natural means. I also could not experience what they described since the chair would not move for me.

I decided to do an EVP session. I asked a number of questions. "Is there anyone here?" "Who is rocking the chair?" "Are you the one talking to the little girl?" "Do you realize you're scaring the parents of the little girl you're talking to?" "Why are you here in this house?" "Was this your house at one time?" Do you need help—is that why you're reaching out to the family?"

I waited after each question to give time for a response. The K-II meter didn't light up during the session at all. The chair hadn't moved either. After a period of silence, I asked if the spirit could move the chair for me. The K-II lit up, but nothing happened. I once again asked if the spirit could move the rocking chair even a little. The K-II lit up again, however, the chair still did not move. "Are you afraid to move the chair for me?" I asked. The K-II lit up and stayed lit for a second. "You don't need to be afraid," I stated. "We're not here because anyone is upset. We just want to know you're here and find out why." Still nothing happened.

I started another EVP session turning off my K-II. My thought was, perhaps the energy the spirit is using to light up the K-II caused him to not have enough energy to move the chair. Whenever a spirit interacts with us, whether it is moving something, touching, speaking, it takes energy. Removing the K-II gives the spirit the opportunity to focus the energy elsewhere.

"I hear you like to talk to the little girl. What do you talk about?" I paused to allow for a response. "The little girl doesn't seem to be afraid of you like her parents are." As I spoke, I noticed the chair twitch. It wasn't a rock, but it did move. I continued to talk about Bernadette. "Bernadette has a nice play set outside. Do you go out to play with her? What is your favorite game to play with the little girl?" The chair moved again. This time it was a bigger swing.

I called the other investigators into the living room. They used their Mel meter, which showed a change of temperature. Around me, the room was a warm 70.2 degrees. On the chair, it was shy of 7 degrees cooler. We all backed away from the rocking chair and gave whatever may have been in the room with us extra space. "Was this your chair?" I asked. I thought back to what Mary Roberts had stated. The activity didn't start until her parents gave her the rocking chair. It is a shared belief in the paranormal field that spirits can attach themselves to items as much as to a place, even going so far as to travel with the item. Perhaps there was a spirit attached to the chair. The rocking chair rocked again. This time we all witnessed it. It was ever so slight of a move, but it was a move.

"Why are you hanging on to the chair?" I asked. After a while longer, the chair stopped moving again, and the Mel meter showed that the temperature near the chair was starting to even out with the rest of the room. It was after two a.m. and it was time to wrap up. We locked up the house as the Roberts requested, and the family friends took the spare keys home with them. Since we promised to share the findings as soon as possible, I got straight to work on uploading the audio and listening to what I may have collected.

The first few questions went unanswered. There was nothing happening until I started talking about little Bernadette. I asked what he talked about with the little girl. There was a male voice that very clearly stated "Stories." When I mentioned that it seemed the little girl wasn't afraid of him, there was a quiet, but audible sounding chuckle. When asked about if he plays with the little girl outside, I got two EVPs: "Swings too high" and "Not safe." When asked about the chair, there was an EVP that was audible, but not as clear as the first EVPs. It sounded as if a man was saying, "My wife's." They were only a few small potential EVPs, but it gave me some insight about what was happening, and perhaps why.

I learned a few things that I was able to bring to the family. The chair may have belonged to the spirit's wife. Mary did tell me that her parents said the chair was handmade as an anniversary gift. Perhaps this was the man who made the chair, and when his wife passed, he clung to it as a way to be close to her. Since I did not know who owned the chair previously, it was just a guess. If it belonged to his wife, the chair must have been important to her, and she must have been important to him. This wasn't a spirit who was there to scare them or hurt them. Perhaps he was attached to the chair, followed the chair to their house, saw Mary was pregnant, and thought he was being helpful by looking out for Bernadette and the baby.

I let them listen to the audio. They were shaken up when I told them I had experiences and heard some electronic voice phenomenon, but once they heard the EVPs for themselves, they seemed to relax. They understood what I meant when I said that it didn't seem the spirit meant harm. I asked about what they thought of the EVP that Bernadette swings too high.

"Tom sometimes puts Bernadette in his lap on the swing and swings with her. I always tell him he's going too high and if he falls off or if the swing breaks (since it's meant for kids not a big man), she's going to get hurt."

"It's obvious your guest thinks so too." I played the audio for her. "He thinks it's unsafe. It seems he worries about Bernadette. The experience your husband had in the baby's nursery may have been the spirit trying to calm the baby until daddy got there." When asked what they should do, I thought for a second. "It's going to be up to you. If you are still bothered by the haunting, talk to the spirit. He obviously was once a person like you and me. Try reasoning with him and tell him that it is scaring you. If you are having issues, feel free to call me again and I can further direct you to other options."

I did receive a call several weeks later from the Roberts. They wanted to give me an update. Tom told me:

"We did as you said. We spoke to the spirit and told him we were afraid when we saw what was happening and didn't know why. Now that we know he wanted to look after us, we wanted to thank him, and tell him that we appreciated his kindness. But we stated that if his wife, who owned the rocking chair, passed away, she was probably lonely waiting for him to cross over and be with her again. The kids would miss him, but it was okay to go if he wanted to be with his wife. After a few days, nothing seemed to happen. Bernadette didn't talk to the chair, the chair didn't rock, and when Daniel started crying to be changed or fed in the middle of the night, he cried until he was clean and had a full belly. It's now been two weeks since anything has happened at all. I think the spirit may have left. I just wanted to say thanks for taking us seriously."

I spoke to the friends of the Roberts family by email and they stated they had been back to the house to do an investigation; they had no reason to believe there was any spirit lingering in the house. It has been quiet ever since. Perhaps that was what the spirit needed—a chance to do something good for someone else, to feel useful, and then be told it was okay to join his beloved wife and be happy. It was also nice that they made the transition easier by thanking him for wanting to help the family while he was there with them. The story started out like a scary ghost story, and ended with a touching, "And they lived happily ever after," paranormal style.

five

The First Ward Schoolhouse

....

Most intelligent spirits were once people just like you or me. Just like some people are friendly, some introverted, some highly active, spirits are the same way. Many times they maintain the personalities they had in life. Unfortunately that means just as some people were mean and evil in life…there are spirits who continue to wreak havoc after life.

The History

The great northern woods has many more places I want to explore and investigate. The more I find, the more I've learned about the paranormal. However, I had a chance to go a little south of the Upper Peninsula to explore another alleged haunting; a much darker haunting. I knew it was an opportunity I couldn't miss out on.

I heard through networks that there was going to be a fundraiser in Wisconsin Rapids, Wisconsin, to save the First Ward Schoolhouse and make necessary repairs. Many of the big names in the paranormal field were scheduled to make an appearance; The Booth Brothers, filmmakers who feature the paranormal in amazing places (such as the Waverly Hills Sanatorium) with movies and documentaries; Ben Hansen, former FBI agent and lead investigator of the hit show *Fact or Faked* on Syfy; Keith Age, the Syfy and Booth Brothers documentary personality; and many more. I read there would also be a chance to do an investigation of the schoolhouse, which is reportedly haunted by a few spirits.

Wisconsin Rapids is a small town in north-central Wisconsin, not far from Stevens Point. It wasn't a long trip, so I jumped at the chance to visit the schoolhouse, especially since it was for such a worthy cause. I made my reservations and started researching the schoolhouse. A helpful friend of the owners, Jenny Gurney, provided me with the history as told to her by the schoolhouse's owners Justin Libigs, Heather Bram, and Judy Carl. According to Jenny, the three did a lot of research on the First Ward by talking to those who lived in the area, doing research at the library, looking through the internet, and talking to the city and the previous owners.

According to Mr. Libigs, in the 1800s Wisconsin Rapids was a budding town. Public schools were becoming overcrowded and thus the board of education decided to open a new school in the first ward district. They found the perfect place for the new school and bought land for $600 from a gentleman named Peter Dessaint. After plans were drawn up, plumbing was put in, construction was done, and essentials such as the bell, seats, and desks were purchased. The total cost of the school came to $10,154. Mr. Libigs noted that one of the more interesting pieces of trivia about the school was that all of its bricks were made on site rather than delivered from a separate location. Also, the doors, gables and classrooms were painted in watercolor.

The school was heated by a giant coal furnace that rested in the basement, and it also adopted the latest in technological advances such as electricity, adjustable seats, and top-of-the-line chalkboards. As of today, First Ward Schoolhouse is the oldest surviving school building still standing in Wisconsin Rapids. The school was made for kindergarten through sixth grade, with the addition of a high school–level grammar class. Physical education was the responsibility of the teachers and taught in the classrooms. The main exception was the janitor, who taught boys basketball in the coal room.

Mr. Libigs mentioned that during a storm in 1910, lightning hit the bell tower, which burned off of the building. They were never able to repair the bell tower, and with the rising costs of maintaining the school (including the $8,000 school tax) the schoolhouse was forced to close its doors.

Justin Libigs is shown here standing beside the bell tower that once sat on top of the school. Photo by Andrea Mesich.

In 1921, schools were once again becoming over-crowded. Catholic nuns in the area decided to save the school and reopen its doors to kindergarten through third grade. The nuns lived in the attic of the school and taught the classes. This kept the cost of running the school down while relieving the overcrowding problem in the lower grades. Shortly after taking the school over in 1921, the roof caught fire due to embers from the coal furnace going up through the chimney and landing hot on the school's roof. The janitor saw the fire on his way home from lunch. No one was injured as all the children were able to get out in time, and because the fire was spotted quickly, the damage was easily repaired.

Before World War II, the building was used as a school for the deaf and was host to the city's first special education classes. Then in 1954, the schoolhouse went through various changes. A kitchen/cafeteria (which also served as a gym) was added, the bathrooms in the basement were moved upstairs, and the coal furnace was upgraded to gas. The last class took place in 1977, and after two years of other use, the building was unused from 1979 until Mr. Libigs and his family heard about the building in 2010, and eventually became owners.

Once the school became the property of Mr. Libigs family and a family friend, unexplainable paranormal activity started happening very quickly. While in the building,

Mr. Libigs and his family were greeted by a male voice saying "Hello." They looked around in wonder, but there was no one else there with them. After that, activity became fairly regular. They heard the sound of desks being moved around the former classrooms; however, there were no school desks left in the building. Many times they heard phantom voices of children and adults. They saw orbs of light and shadow figures with the naked eye, and heard footsteps coming from places where no one was walking around. It was later that Mr. Libigs found out they were not the first to claim paranormal activity in the schoolhouse. It was the nuns who first noted unexplainable phenomenon in the 1920s.

Looking into the potential hauntings, there are a few claims that need researching. The first is that there is a little girl seen in a few places. One is the attic where a little girl can be heard crying. A little girl has also been seen in the former classroom on the second floor. Then there are various sounds of children and the sound of desks that no longer exist in the building moving. Neighbors have said they have seen an old man in the third-floor window; there is also an angry older gentleman (possibly the same as seen on the third floor) who spends a lot of time in the basement, specifically the coal room. It also seems the little girl is not the only child spirit.

When talking to those involved with the First Ward, I found that the only known deaths at the school were a

little boy named Oscar, who allegedly died in the building from a cause that remains unknown, and the little
girl mentioned earlier, who (it has been said) was killed
in a tragic accident in front of the school sometime in the
1930s. With only two documented deaths in or near the
schoolhouse, why were the other spirits there? How did
they return to the school after death? Is it possible that
perhaps whatever spirit had an attachment to the school
was buried in a nearby cemetery and returned? Looking
around, I found two cemeteries within one mile of the
schoolhouse: Forest Hill Cemetery and Calvary Cemetery. Both cemeteries have graves from the late 1800s
to the early 1900s. Could some of those graves contain
the remains of students or teachers of the First Ward
Schoolhouse who walked that mile back to the school?

   While I was at the First Ward, there were people
gossiping about dark things that happened at the school.
Since I have found nothing to substantiate the claims I
won't mention what those alleged dark things were, but
if those things did occur, could the perpetrator be bound
to the site for the crimes committed, unable to move on?

   A while back, I had the chance to speak to a Catholic
priest who was very open to the belief in the paranormal;
he gave me another theory as to why spirits who may not
have specifically died in or near a place they now haunt,
may linger there. When asked his thoughts, he stated
that like many, he didn't have the answers; however, one

of his beliefs stands in the Catholic theory of a place called purgatory.

In the Catholic faith, purgatory is a place of temporal punishment for those who died in God's grace to purify themselves of sins they may not have had a chance to repent for before their passing. Purgatory derives from a Latin word meaning "to purify." It is a place a spirit goes to fully repent or pay to the satisfaction of their transgressions. Where this place is, no one knows.

Could it be possible that the spirit is allowed to linger in a place that has meaning to them, whether good or bad, during this time? Perhaps what we feel as ghosts haunting an area, are actually spirits in purgatory. If you notice in many investigations, when asked if spirits need help moving on, many times they say "Yes." Could this be because they are unsure how to end their purgatory? Purgatory could also be for those who do not understand they are dead, or cannot let go of their worldliness and move on. So while they are not unworthy of God's love and grace, they cannot move on until they have accepted and purified themselves.

On the flip side, it is a strong belief of the priest's that demons do exist. Many times they attach themselves to places where dark things happened. Sometimes dark forces allow the spirit of someone who did evil things in life to remain where those evils were done so that they could continue to try to lead God's children astray, and/or wreak havoc on lives. Of course, this is only one of many theories he has about the paranormal.

Could the priest's theory be right? Could good spirits be in purgatory? Perhaps they need to cleanse themselves of venial sins, stuck in the place where those sins occurred, or they may not know they are deceased or are unable to allow themselves to let go of this world? Could dark forces be attracted to places where dark things occurred, or could the spirit that created the dark events be forced to return to where those evils happened?

There was a lot to consider for reasons a spirit would linger in a place where they did not die. The priest said it could be a place they were attached to in life—good or bad—whether it was a sort of purgatory or a place to continue to do the evils they had started while alive. Another theory came from a seminar I attended.

I had the honor to ask Jason Hawes and Grant Wilson (from *Ghost Hunters* on Syfy) a question when they spoke in Milwaukee, Wisconsin, and they gave me some more food for thought. Most intelligent spirits were humans once. We humans travel, we move from place to place freely. If spirits were once human, who is to say they don't continue these same habits of traveling and moving about from place to place?

Another theory is that if they have an attachment to an item, they will follow that item where it goes. Could a spirit in the building have been attached to an item in life they took with them from the school that made its way back and they followed it? If they had an attachment to the property and are buried nearby, it isn't far-fetched to believe the spirit would travel the short distance from one of the cemeteries nearby back to the school. Jason and Grant believe there is no reason a spirit can't roam the way they roamed in life.

So even though Oscar and the little girl are the only deaths related to the school, there are many reasons and ways spirits would occupy the property.

Everyone who heard about the upcoming fundraiser started going online to share their stories about investigations at the schoolhouse. I spoke to nineteen-year-old Jenny Gurney, who shared her experiences at the First Ward with me.

"I have been interested in the paranormal for about five years, ever since I began watching *Ghost Hunters*. I officially joined the field two years ago by attending Parasota 2010, that Brandy Green hosted. Ever since, I have been busy within the paranormal field, attending several conventions and meeting people within the field. I'm so grateful for meeting everyone I have met in the paranormal community. I have investigated two of the biggest haunts in the United States; Waverly Hills and Bobby Mackey's, both with Justin Libigs and Judy Carl. But I have also investigated the Palmer House Hotel in

Minnesota, Farrar School in Iowa, Morrison Lodge in Kentucky, and many other amazing haunted locations.

This past year I started my own paranormal team, Proximity Paranormal, out of Minnesota with a great group of friends. I have also started my own paranormal radio show, *Paranormal Hotspot* (on Ztalkradio.com) on Wednesdays at ten p.m. Eastern time. I'm looking forward to see where the paranormal field will take me in the future.

I met the owner of the schoolhouse and his family many years ago via a mutual friend. We met in person for the first time at the Parasota convention, and ever since we have been great friends and even became family. I think of Justin as my para-brother because since we met he has always watched out for me and protected me from bad forces on paranormal investigations. It was an exciting opportunity for me when I got to go to Wisconsin Rapids to see the schoolhouse Justin and his family purchased, and finally investigate it. My first thoughts on the schoolhouse as I pulled up to it was, holy crap, it is huge. The schoolhouse itself gives off a somewhat creepy vibe, like you just know it's haunted and there are things happening in it. I fell in love with the schoolhouse the first time I laid eyes on the building.

After my first encounter, I have been to the schoolhouse about ten times. The schoolhouse has became my second home, and I always have a open invite to come and stay. I also book the investigations for the schoolhouse for Justin and the other owners when teams want to come in. I was one of the people who helped set up this particular fundraiser that you came to, in order to raise some money for the restoration that Justin is doing. I try to help the school as much as I can because I love it so much. This schoolhouse is a hidden treasure in the Midwest.

The first thing that pops into my head when it comes to experiences at the schoolhouse would have to be my lock-in in the coal room in the basement. This was a bet that Justin gave me; if I could last one hour in the coal room, I would get $60. He didn't believe I could last one hour alone in the very haunted room. I wanted to prove him wrong, so I accepted. This was a true lock-in; Justin locked me in where the only way out was with a key. He set up a camera in the coal room so he could keep an eye on me. After he locked me in, he left the basement with no flashlights, no lights of any kind, and no gear at all. The only thing I had was a voice recorder and the video camera he placed in the room. No one was on the floor above me or the floor above that. Everyone else was in the attic investigating.

Not even five minutes after he left, all hell broke loose. I kept hearing footsteps outside the room and other noises. Then I kept hearing noises within the coal room, which is when I started to freak out. I saw a full-body apparition in front of my face, moving toward the camera; that is when the camera became disconnected from the cord. It is the type of cord that locks when you connect it, and you have to unlock it before disconnecting, so it would take a lot of energy to do it.

As the full-body apparition moved closer to me, I freaked out, then it disappeared. That's when I heard banging on the door from the outside, like it was trying to open the door. Justin came down because he saw the camera was disconnected. When he came to the basement, he saw that the door was pulled out. He thought it was me, but it wasn't. He left the coal room and the noises continued, the door being opened, banging on the washer/dryer, footsteps. Suddenly, the light in the main basement room turned on, and then shut off, I thought it was Justin playing a joke on me. I kept seeing feet in the crack of the door. These noises kept happening for over an hour, and it turns out, it wasn't Justin. I think the spirit of the janitor was trying to get into the room. I'm not sure who was the spirit IN the room with me was, but it was a child's height.

On other investigations I have done at the schoolhouse, we have caught full-body apparitions in the attic, the basement and a couple of times in the other rooms. We have heard voices, and interaction with spirits in many different ways. The spirit of the little girl, Betty, loves to come out and play with us. She loves to dance and sing when we sing children's songs. The spirit of the janitor loves to come out in the basement when down there. There are also spirits of teachers and other children seen and heard throughout the school.

In 2012, new spirits entered the school. Justin and the family bought two beds from the famous Lemp Mansion and we think a couple of the spirits came with the beds. We have made contact with two males. We aren't sure yet exactly who they are, but we believe they were part of the Lemp family.

The spirits at the schoolhouse love the spirit box, flashlights, and toys (especially the spirits of the children). They love to communicate with the flashlights.

After speaking to Jenny about the history of the First Ward, I did some research on the beds from the Lemp Mansion. The Lemp Mansion has a tragic and haunted history, a history that could cause the possibility of spiritual attachment to occur, bringing those spirits into the First Ward.

The Lemp Mansion is a reportedly haunted mansion in St. Louis, Missouri, a site of sadness and tragedy. William J. Lemp Sr.'s favored son Fredrick became ill and passed away at the young age of twenty-eight. Soon after, a close friend also passed away. William Sr. suffered for three years with depression and eventually committed suicide by gunshot in 1904. The youngest daughter of William Sr., Elsa, married a man named Thomas from whom she would ultimately file for divorce. They reconciled in March of 1920, but that reconciliation ended when she shot herself later that month. In 1922, William Sr.'s son, William Jr., committed suicide by gunshot in the house due to marital and business issues that plagued him when he took over the family business upon his father's suicide. Charles Lemp, another son of William Sr., lived in the mansion with his dog. In 1949, he shot his dog before committing suicide himself. The only surviving son of William Sr. was Edwin, who died of natural causes at the age of ninety. Most of the suicides, as well as other deaths related to the Lemp family, took place in the actual mansion. The owners of the First Ward believe one of the beds they have is either a bed where a suicide took place, or where the body was laid after.

It was an interesting story, and made the First Ward Schoolhouse even more compelling and I was greatly looking forward to seeing the place for myself.

The Investigation

On a warm afternoon in late September, I arrived at the First Ward Schoolhouse to attend a fundraiser to help with restoration of the historical building. It was a much larger building that I had anticipated seeing. I ran my hand against the rough red brick and looked at the names scratched into the walls. I saw names like Sarah, Nikki,

Matty; names from 1992 and names dated 1952. The giant dome that used to be on the top of the schoolhouse was now resting in front of it. It was so large even a tall 6-foot, 4-inch man like *Fact or Faked*'s Ben Hanson looked miniscule in comparison. The building looked old, yet it held up well over the years. Minus typical wear and tear issues, it still stood strong and proud in its little corner of Wisconsin Rapids.

The house was bigger than I imagined it would be. When walking in, there was an entryway with stairs that led to the second floor and down to the basement. Walking through a doorway to the left of the stairs, there was the large room that was originally the kindergarten room when the schoolhouse was still in action. If you head to the back of the kindergarten room, you will find another set of stairs up to the second floor and down to the basement. The second floor has a few former classrooms that are now being used as bedrooms. One room on the second floor contains the beds that were brought over from the Lemp Mansion. Another room, which was locked to the general public, originally a music room, was thoroughly soundproofed so as to not disturb other classes. This room became another bedroom used by the owners. There is also a large attic, a very large basement with a room that served as a cafeteria and gym, and the infamous coal room where much of the paranormal activity seems to occur.

In the kindergarten room, there were many tables set up for the guests of honor and other merchants who were there throughout the day during the fundraiser. I met Tina Anderson, a jeweler selling bracelets, earrings, and necklaces made from precious stones such as agates. I purchased a beautiful purple-colored agate necklace from her that I still wear today. It has turned into a good-luck charm of sorts for me.

I also had the great honor to meet filmmakers Christopher Saint Booth and his brother Philip Adrian Booth. They make great movies and documentaries such as *Death Tunnel*, *Children of the Grave*, *Children of the Grave II*, *Spooked*, *The Possessed*, *The Unseen*, and *The Haunted Boy*, all of which are available on DVD at spookedtv.com. The documentaries such as *Children of the Grave I & II*, *Spooked* and *The Unseen* show some of the most frightening and sad tales of the lives lost that still stick around. The fact that the stories are all true, the EVPs you hear are real, and the photos you see are unedited; makes the documentaries all the more intense. The Booth brothers expertly convey the deepest of emotion, raw and real, through their work. Their passion comes through each of their projects. It was an exciting moment to meet them face to face.

Having seen so many of their movies and documentaries, this was a big honor for me. I was able to stand next to the makers of these documentaries that made me tear up, gave me the chills, and made me jump, all at the same time.

The author with the Booth brothers and Keith Age.
Photo courtesy of Andrea Mesich.

That first day I had requested a reading from psychics Scotty Rorek and Deb Lantz out of curiosity. We went into the backyard of the First Ward in the sunlight and peaceful quiet of that warm September day. The first thing Scotty said to me before we even sat down is that he didn't know why I approached him for a reading. He stated that he clearly saw a wall built up around me that showed him I didn't believe in psychics or psychic abilities. When he asked Deb to join him, he kept telling her that it was odd that I wanted a reading even though I thought this was all bunk. He was right about that. Being honest, I planned on proving a point by not giving any information to him or Deb that could be used to do what is called a "cold reading."

Cold readings are used by alleged psychics to elicit information needed from the subject of the reading without their knowledge in order to make it appear they are seeing things they are not. For example, a psychic may say "I see a J, someone with a J…Jason, Janice, Jake, Janelle…it is with a J…" the person may say, "My father is John" and from there the psychic could ask, "Is your father deceased?" If the person says yes, the psychic can run from there to make it appear they are speaking to that spirit.

I had every intention of making sure I did not allow for cold readings, so Scotty's initial thought was very interesting. But we went ahead with it. Both he and Deb made mention of a good number of things that they would not have prior knowledge of. Scotty knew instantly that I was a writer even though no one at the convention knew why I was there. He also knew I was having some issues with a few chapters due to skepticism. He stated the words would flow easier if I kept a healthy amount of skepticism, but lowered the wall just a bit. I had to stop denying my experiences or looking for reasons they occurred and just accept them for what they were. If I were able to do that, to be honest with myself and my readers, the words would just flow. Deb hit on a few personal things, again, I can't imagine how anyone would know. I barely said a word as to not give hints. I was very surprised.

What I enjoyed most was that they did not talk to me about the future, and they didn't tell me to buy their books or call a 1-900 number for more information—they talked to me about what they saw of my personality and my past, and how to use that to make a better present, be a better me, which will help me in the future. The conversation was uplifting. I left with a little less skepticism. It was an interesting meeting. I hold one proud title: Deb said I am the only one to date who didn't cry during the readings. Apparently, people cry during readings. Perhaps I was too fascinated.

There were many interesting people at the convention. I ran into Jenny Gurney (who provided the history of the schoolhouse) and her mother, Bonnie. I also met a demonologist, the owners of the schoolhouse, psychics, a spiritual artist, paranormal radio-show hosts, other paranormal investigators. Everywhere I turned, there were new and interesting people to meet.

I had the pleasure of meeting another psychic medium, Justin Chase Mullins, who later shared with me his thoughts on the First Ward after the fundraiser came to a close. I asked him to share with me his experiences as an investigator and then as a psychic medium.

This is based upon just evidence, and not my role as a psychic medium. I was in the basement, my friend

Daniel and I did an EVP session. I said I am Justin Chase Mullins, I'm a psychic and medium. Give me a sign of your presence. We captured an EVP of a growl and then a light bulb in the next room exploded, which we were able to capture evidence of.

Later, we investigated the attic. In leaving the attic, I heard my name said out loud. I had a lot of spirit box EVPs from the classroom upstairs, with the boards. I proclaimed that I am Mr. Mullins, the new teacher. There was lots of aggressive EVP responses to that. I feel like there's still such an authority there, one that punished the kids cruelly and hurt them through punishment. I just got the vibe I couldn't shake that the children were hurt.

Speaking as a psychic medium now, prior to coming to the location, they called so I could do a reading without having a chance to investigate the place. I picked up on wooden floors, an attic, upstairs, there is a man near the window on the left. He appears as a shadow and looms over. He did bad things there. He died at the location, upstairs. There was also another death of a heart attack. There's a boy spirit and a girl spirit who linger around each other. Also present are a dominant male authority faculty member who still rules the school and a singular female who is very strict. The children had harsh punishment and some of the authority figures were abusive.

When I asked if the spirit Justin saw dying at the location upstairs was the same darker entity that is often seen or felt in the basement, he stated: "Yes, the basement is borderline demonic, very dark. I got sick from being there. The classroom on the left on the second floor has a dominant male teacher also." So in Justin Chase Mullin's beliefs, there were more deaths in the house, though no documentation has been found.

The fundraiser had a number of events going on: psychic readings, psychic artistry, and sales of ghost hunting DVDs, books, and investigative equipment. There was also a silent auction with jewelry and items donated by various paranormal celebrities and local businesses to help raise money for the First Ward. Two deejays, Joe and Kale, from a show called *The Skeptical Edge*, were broadcasting live on location.

However, I was most interested in the investigation that would happen later that night, and the next. I spent the day talking to the Booth Brothers, a little more to Scotty Rorek and Tina Anderson, then I headed back to my hotel for a quick rest. After a nap, evening was quickly growing, and the investigation was about to begin. I made sure I had all of my equipment with me. My K-II meter was in perfect working order, my Mel meter and both of my recorders had brand-new batteries. I packed them up in a backpack and headed back to the First Ward.

At the beginning of the night, we divided up into small groups and each took turns in different locations. One group went to the bedroom on the second floor, one went to the basement, one went into the kindergarten room, and my group headed first to the attic. The plan would be to stay in a location for an hour, then rotate down. When we'd go to the second-floor bedroom, the team in that bedroom would then go down to the kindergarten room, and so on.

While in the attic, I placed my recorders in various places, set the K-II meter down where I could see it, and then held my Mel meter to check for any fluctuations in temperature. The unfortunate thing about the attic was the echo. You could hear everything that was going on in the lower levels, no matter how quiet they were trying to be. When we heard a knock, the knock could have been from a spirit or from someone in the second-floor bedroom or the kindergarten room. Whispers could have been coming from anywhere.

Justin Chase Mullins decided to do a spirit box session. A spirit box (or ghost box) is a modified portable AM/FM radio that scans the band nonstop, creating, in essence, nothing more than white noise and audio remnants from broadcast stations. Entities are able to use those remnants and the white noise to form words in response to questions. It is a highly debated piece of equipment; the main issue is, you cannot completely rule out explainable causes for responses, such as a station broadcast briefly coming through, or CB radio interference. This is why the investigators using this device at the First Ward would often ask a spirit to use the spirit box to say a certain swear word that would not be allowed on the air due to FCC regulations. Sometimes they would tell the spirit their name, and ask the spirit to repeat it a few times in a row.

Due to the sound coming from below, I had a hard time concentrating on the session and didn't pick up on much of what was being said. I simply kept my eyes on my Mel and my K-II, and whispered a few questions of my own, hoping to pick something up on my digital recorders. It seemed nothing was happening. The Mel didn't go off and the K-II didn't even light up from natural EMFs—there was simply nothing. The hour went by fairly quickly, and it was time to head to the next room. I took as many pictures as I could before leaving, but I just had the sense that if anything was there, it did not want to make itself known.

My group headed to the second-floor bedroom. Minus the beds, it still very much had the appearance of a classroom. I took one of the smaller beds; Jenny Gurney, who was in the group, and another investigator sat on the larger bed. Justin Chase Mullins and a few other investigators sat at a table in the middle of the room, while two women and one of their husbands took chairs in the corner. The two women were sisters. I learned this when I thought one of the women said something aimed at me, before she apologized and stated she was saying it to her sister.

The attic of the First Ward Schoolhouse.
Photo by Andrea Mesich.

One sister found a skeleton dressed in a white robe toy on a string, and started teasing the other sister with it. They started giggling. As they joked around with the toy, my K-II meter started spiking intermittently. It was odd; it hadn't moved since I sat down. The Mel meter's temperature gauge started showing a minor drop in temperature, nothing that would have sparked my attention. I chalked it up to normal fluctuations in natural EMF and temperature. The spirits of children are known to appear in the second-floor room, especially the little girl. We prepared to reach out to her and any other spirit willing to speak with us.

Justin Chase Mullins took some time to get a feel for the room. He made mention of the larger bed, stating he saw odd energy around it—as if someone had died in the bed. He said this with no prior knowledge that the bed was said to be one of the beds from the Lemp Mansion, where multiple family members took their own lives. As he explained what he felt he was seeing, the K-II meter started to light up again, and once again the Mel had a minimal drop in temperature; just not enough that I thought it would be of significance.

Eventually we switched around, those of us on the beds switched with those at the tables. The second I sat at the table instead of the bed, the K-II and Mel meter became silent. We once again pulled out the spirit box, but our hour was coming to a close, and it was time to move on to the kindergarten room, so we decided against another session. As we moved from the attic to the second floor, I noticed a notable drop in sound interference. The noise wasn't as frequent and the noise wasn't nearly as loud, which made things a lot easier. The same went for the kindergarten room. It seemed the echoes and noise dulled each floor down.

There were rumors of children spirits in the kindergarten room. One investigator stated he had been there before and was able to get the children to communicate with them by playing games and promising they could go outside to play. He did say there is a spirit they refer to as "the Shepherd," who keeps the children from leaving. He encountered issues with the Shepherd during that investigation. The children seemed to be responding, things were being felt and heard at that moment, K-II meters were going off, and EVPs were caught; then everything stopped as it seemed like a darker force entered the room. They believe it was the Shepherd stopping the children from going outside to play when they opened the doors as promised.

After some time in the kindergarten room, I decided to step up and take the reins in the EVP session. I took my Mel and K-II meters and placed them in front of me, and started asking questions. There was candy in a candy dish on the table from the fundraiser earlier that day. I told the children if they'd play a game with me, they would get candy, and I placed the candy near the meters. I explained that the K-II meter was like a carnival game. At a carnival there is a game where you take a big mallet and hit a lever with all your might, and however high the ball inside the game goes up is how strong you are. There are words like puny, mouse, weakling, muscle man, and at the very top if you ding the bell, you're the ultimate strong man. The K-II is like that. The higher up a spirit can make the lights go, the stronger they are, and they win a prize; some candy.

Just at that moment, the K-II meter went all the way to red, and the Mel meter, for the first time, not only displayed a noted difference in temperature, the built-in EMF detector, which was at a constant 0.0 had gone up to a 3.0. Had a spirit communicated with us? Suddenly, another investigator joined the room, and closed the door behind him. We all continued our EVP work and were discussing occurrences of the past with the investigator who had already been to the location, when suddenly the door opened on its own, several minutes later!

I looked out in the hall to see a gentleman standing there. He said he saw the door open and assumed someone was leaving. Later, we discovered if the door isn't properly latched, someone walking by the doors that lead outside opening and closing could cause enough pressure for the door to open. The investigator was positive the door was completely and properly shut, but we decided it was explainable and continued the investigation.

The hour was almost up and nothing more seemed to be happening. It was almost as if a heavier presence in the room came in the second the equipment started activating. Could a child spirit have been playing with us, and this Shepherd spirit stopped them from communicating? Perhaps the door wasn't merely a coincidence. Maybe the Shepherd walked in and took the child away from us, as that was the moment the activity stopped.

Now it was time to head down to the basement. I was looking forward to this. We first went into the room that they were using earlier in the day for lectures. When the building was a school, this was the cafeteria that doubled as a gym. The first thing everyone noticed was a phantom smell, the smell of wood burning, or maybe like someone smoking a pipe. However, there was a bonfire earlier in the evening, and many speculated the smell was remnants of the fire. It is always good to think about and exhaust logical explanations first because that improves potential evidence collected. We felt that phantom smell, while not 100 percent positive, could be explained by natural means. Many people stated they saw an unexplained colored light in the back of the room, but not much else of note happened.

Finally, we were able to get into the coal room. I was looking forward to it. One of the previous groups mentioned that a female investigator was scratched. They could see the scratches forming on her arm right before their eyes. She felt the burning, so they put a flashlight over her arm, and the red marks started to appear at the top, and headed down toward her wrist. I knew this was going to be interesting. When we walked into the coal room, it was immediately apparent why people were "creeped out." It seemed they kept all of the Halloween decorations in that room. Rubber evil clown masks, a giant rubber spider, a Frankenstein monster statue—it was cool and frightening at the same time.

The previous group had set up chairs, so after some small talk we each took one and closed the door. The room was relatively small. I couldn't imagine anyone practicing basketball in the coal room as stated in the history. Someone started to explain a little about the room and the things that happen in there. As she spoke, I could feel things getting very heavy—literally heavy, as if someone was stacking bricks on top of my shoulders. I could feel the pressure as it weighed me down; word by word as she spoke, the heaviness became more intense. I tried to concentrate on what was being said, which was that the center of the wall to my left is said to be a portal or vortex for spirits to travel through. Some called it the gateway to hell since it seemed there was such a dark spirit in the coal room.

I didn't get the entire conversation as I started to feel even heavier at the mention of the gateway to hell. My Mel meter was starting to show a drop in temperature and a slight spike in EMFs. I didn't say anything right away. I didn't want anyone to get worried. Suddenly, I was having trouble breathing. Many times people who experience the paranormal say they feel as if they have had the wind knocked out of them, but this was not the case for me. I actually felt my throat tightening, like something was grasping me by the neck. Someone noticed the color leaving my face and asked if I was all right. I passed it off and said I was fine, but I could still feel my throat tightening. You could almost feel four fingers on one side and a thumb on the other. I could see the Mel meter next to my feet still dropping in temperature and the EMF had spiked to 5, the highest I've ever seen it go. The feeling was heavy, dark, and angry. Something was angry at ME!

Finally, I had had enough and it was time to make the feeling stop. Going to my Catholic training, in my mind I started saying the "Our Father" prayer, and making the sign of the cross on my knee with my finger. As I did this, the feeling eased up around my neck, but the heaviness did not leave the room right away. Again, someone asked me if I was okay. I simply asked, "Did anyone else feel it get really heavy in here just now, like just dark and heavy?" Suddenly there was a collective sigh around the room as if everyone was saying, "Thank God it wasn't just me." It seemed people were a little cautious about speaking up, probably out of fear of being looked at oddly. Now that I had finally said something, they knew it was okay. I explained what I just experienced, when someone else spoke up and said she was having issues breathing, but wasn't sure what to think. Her issues started almost immediately after mine stopped. A man stood up and declared that he was done and needed to get out of the room immediately. His wife stood up shortly after and said she was done too. "This room isn't right" was all she said as she exited.

At that point, no one was sure if they wanted to stay. I wanted to. I needed to stay and figure out what was going on; however, if everyone else was leaving, what was I to do? One brave soul spoke up and said that she was going to stay alone if she had to. While several people did leave to join other groups, those of us who were curious enough stayed with her. Eventually the deejay from the radio show, Joe, joined us in the coal room. After he settled, without warning, a basketball came rolling between me and the girl sitting to my right. It rolled forward a little ways, then stopped. There was no logical explanation why it suddenly rolled out. I could see when someone came in or left opening and closing the door behind them or when people were moving around, but that was happening the whole time I was there. People were moving around, leaving, entering, and the ball never moved. I was unaware there was even a ball in the room until that second. It wasn't until he entered, sat against the wall, and we were all settled and about to start an EVP session again that it rolled out. How strange was it that it was a basketball in this former basketball room?

We explained to Joe what happened before he came, the feeling of anger in the room, the hand around my throat, and the couple leaving as fast as they could. When he was brought up to speed, we started an EVP session. Joe spoke up immediately and asked if there was an oppressive spirit present, and what issue they had with people. We paused, and I continued the question asking if the issue was with women. There was a man in the room previously before he decided to leave, yet it seemed the two who had issues were myself and another female. So it seemed to go straight for women. We continued on like this for some time.

The hour was up, and it was nearing four a.m., the end of the first night of investigation. I knew that come the next night of investigations, I'd want to be down in the coal room for the majority of the evening. I headed back to my hotel after cleansing myself with a few prayers and insisting no spirit was allowed to follow me. When I reached the hotel, I got into bed and immediately fell asleep.

The next day I went back to the fundraiser where I had the honor of meeting Mr. Ben Hansen—former FBI agent, and star of the hit Syfy series *Fact or Faked: Paranormal Files*. Ben was going to be a guest investigator during the second night of investigations, and I was looking forward to seeing his techniques and possibly learning a few new things about investigating the paranormal from a professional. Of course, being a fan of Mr. Hansen and his show, I made sure to stop and get an autographed photo as well as take the opportunity to get a photo with Ben for my scrapbook. For those who haven't met him in person, he is a very tall man, standing 6-foot-4 at least. I jokingly asked the gentleman who took the photo if he was able to get all of Ben in it. Mr. Hansen was extremely friendly at the convention and had a nice word for everyone he met.

Ben Hansen gave an excellent lecture to those attending the
fundraiser at First Ward. Photo by Andrea Mesich.

Later in the afternoon, I had the chance to listen to one of Ben's lectures on the paranormal and specifically, the extraterrestrial. It was an extremely thought-provoking seminar. He showed things from a point of view that would even make skeptics take notes. It was a fresh perspective on some cases I already knew about, but had been skeptical about, until his lecture showed me a few things I needed to rethink. His lecture showed his knowledge on the subject of the paranormal and extraterrestrial, which made me look forward to seeing his advice for paranormal investigations. I had a feeling that with Mr. Hansen's expertise, I would learn about new devices or investigation techniques I could use in my own research. However, Mr. Hansen had to wait. I needed to get back to the coal room one more time.

After having dinner, and getting a quick nap in, it was time for the second night of the investigation. This time I started in the coal room. I joined a group with two girls and a few gentlemen. When we first got to the room, we whispered quietly about how we would tackle the investigation. It was decided that two of the gentleman would enter a crawlspace that is said to be extremely active, while the rest of us went into the coal room and shut ourselves in. Someone in the group made the suggestion that of us girls, one should go into the hall alone, as the spirit of the angry man seems to make himself known to females specifically. I immediately jumped at the chance to investigate the hall on my own hoping the spirit would make himself known.

Not even a few minutes into standing in the hall, my K-II started to go off; it went off all the way to red. I did an EMF sweep and found two places several feet away where there were consistent spikes in EMF near wiring. Using my Mel meter, I noticed the EMFs were minimal—not enough for me to consider the spikes on the K-II as anything but natural or man-made.

One of the girls from the group joined me in the hall and showed me a few places to test with the K-II and the Mel to see if EMF spikes they were getting back in the coal room could be explained. At the end of the hall was a room. The doorway was open, but there were no lights on, so it was dark inside the room. As we were about to head back into the coal room to sweep the room for consistent EMFs, something drew my eyes toward that room at the end of the hall.

A figure from within the dark room had appeared in the doorway, into the lighted area near the hall; it stopped to look directly at me. I can see the figure now as clearly as I saw it then, but it remains difficult to describe. I could see arms; one arm by its side, the other holding onto the frame of the doorway as if bracing itself. I could see the head, which slowly tilted to one side in an inquisitive manner. I saw it was standing on two legs; I could see how short it was based on how far up it stood in the doorway. It was definitely shorter that myself (I am 5-foot-7). It was too short to be anyone in my current group. I could see the shape of the clothes the "person" was wearing. The top, whatever or whoever it was, was wearing was white, and I could see the shape of the hair. However I didn't see facial features—no eyes, no nose, no mouth, nothing that would define the figure as a child or adult other than the height, which could have been the height of a child. The face was blank. The figure also wasn't solid. It had a translucent look, almost as if you'd be able to see right through into the room. After a few seconds of staring at each other in awe, it quickly ducked back into the room as if running away from my gaze.

I immediately pointed out what I had seen to the member I was standing with, and we ran into the room to see if anyone was there—a stray investigator from another group, or anyone. We reached the room in seconds and it was empty. There was nothing in that room. Even more, I noted there was no way in or out of the room except for the doorway in which we came.

I searched for a panel, a door, anything that someone could have come and gone through without having to pass by us. The only way out was the doorway where it stood for those few moments. So if it were an actual person, it should have still been in the room, but there was nothing in the room at all. To this day, I still think about what I saw. I can see it even now as I close my eyes, and I still get chills up my spine. It was there. We looked at each other long enough for me to know it was really there, and I know that whatever it was, it was looking back at me with eyes I couldn't see. There is no doubt in my mind.

After a few moments of looking around, trying to figure out what was going on, we headed back to the coal room. We began another EVP session. One investigator began to ask if the spirit wanted me to go back into the hall alone. As she was asking, the girl who came into the hall with me asked if she should volunteer to go out alone instead. The male investigator with us asked in a low and quiet voice, "You'd do that?" This investigator had admitted she was feeling really scared at the moment, so it wasn't something we expected her to offer.

Before we could decide who should return alone into the hall, the gentlemen who were in the crawlspace appeared in the room. They were pale white and out of breath and had beads of sweat dripping from their brows. They stated that they needed to get out of there. One anxiously said they had come face to face with a really bad entity, and they started to feel as if something was taking over their emotions. One explained that he started feeling angry, an emotion he rarely felt. It scared him and they just had to get out. You could see by the looks on their faces and the trembling of their hands that they were not exaggerating. They were dead serious. I wasn't one to doubt them after what I had just seen not too long before.

After a while we regrouped and divided up. Some of our group went to investigate a small utility closet at the end of the basement, while one investigator and I stayed in the coal room alone. She took out her spirit box and started a session. There was a constant voice coming through, and it didn't sound friendly. A few times we heard a few "F" words (which would not be allowed on the radio). The more we got the unfriendly voice, the more the other investigator started to complain that she wasn't feeling well. Finally we heard a different voice come through. It said "Help." My fellow investigator and I looked at each other.

"Are you a different spirit?" My K-II meter lit up for the first time in the room as we heard what sounded like a "yes" come through the spirit box. "Were you the one trying to communicate to us for help and we were thinking you were the angry spirit?" The K-II lit up again. "We're sorry. We didn't know it was you," I stated. "So are you alone now?" Suddenly, without explanation, a flashlight belonging to someone in the group turned on. The flashlight was sitting there, unused for the last hour—no one touched it, it had not moved, or rolled, nor had it been bumped—yet suddenly it was on. "If you turned the flashlight on, can you turn it off again to let us know?" The flashlight turned off.

It suddenly got very cold behind my back. So cold, I actually took notice of it. It had been a solid 70 degrees according to my Mel meter from the moment we had come into the coal room. Now, as the flashlight seemed to turn on and off at command, the temperature around me dropped to 63 degrees, a little shy of the 10-degree drop that clearly indicates activity. I felt the wall behind me; it was cold as ice. One thing I should note about the wall—I was sitting against the wall that on the previous night had been called the gateway to hell.

I decided to ask another question. "Do you really need help?" There was skepticism in my voice. Something didn't feel right to me. Nothing happened. No K-II, no flashlight, nothing. So I asked again, "Is the spirit with us in need of help?" Nothing happened again. No K-II, no flashlight. The cold spot seemed to be moving now. I felt as if I was starting to feel warmth again. The temperature near me was now 69 degrees and the wall was not cold against my back. However, the temperature near the other investigator was starting to cool down. We asked if whatever was in the room was just messing with us, pretending to be in need of help as a joke; the flashlight turned on, and the temperature dropped to 66.6 degrees. I took that as either the spirit playing a cruel joke on us, tugging at our heart strings, or there was a spirit there looking for help, and this darker entity took over and suppressed it like the shepherd in the kindergarten room the night before.

Eventually the other investigator had to leave, but left the flashlight in my hands as the next group came down. In the next group, one of the Booth Brothers and another investigator, Keith Age, who has worked with the Booths on many occasions, joined us in the basement. They passed around new equipment that I hadn't worked with before, taught us how to use it and gave us the opportunity to put it into action. However, back in the coal room now with Judy Carl joining me briefly, nothing much seemed to happen except floating cold spots. It was 70 degrees, and when asked to make the temperature drop, it dropped into the mid-60s. Once again it seemed to float, it was pacing between those of us in the room.

When I started to feel warmer, Judy spoke up, saying she felt it getting colder by her.

When the cold spot was on you, despite it being in the 60s, which isn't freezing cold, you felt chilled to the bone. I could feel my body shaking and my teeth chattered, it was a very physical reaction. However, that seemed to be all that happened, and even after a while, that stopped. The flashlight hadn't gone off since the last incident, and none of the other equipment seemed to be getting any responses. There was no feeling of a presence in the room. It was quiet.

We joined Keith Age in the main room of the basement and discussed what happened. We had a debate about the flashlight, we discussed other equipment, orbs in photos, and investigation techniques. I felt the more we spoke, the more I felt the pressure lifting. I hadn't even realized that pressure was there until I started to feel so much more relaxed. It was getting toward the end of the night and there were two more rooms left to do in a short time. I decided to head up to the second-floor bedroom and use that time to investigate with Ben Hansen of *Fact or Faked*.

When I walked upstairs, Ben Hansen was sitting at the table working on a contraption with a little LED light. I sat down at the table with him and Tina Anderson, the jeweler I had purchased my necklace from. I placed my recorders down in front of me, as well as the K-II and Mel meters. Owner Justin Libigs stopped by and gave a little history about the room, how the little girl seems to frequent the room the most; she has been physically seen, and heard without need of equipment. Once he finished telling us the history, he said goodbye and then left us to it. The lights went out, and Ben explained his device. Fixing it up just so, he explained that with just a simple touch, or bump, the light would be activated. His theory was, with just a little energy, even a weaker spirit would be able to communicate by turning on the light. He tested it a few times to make sure it was functioning properly. Everything seemed to be in working order.

It was unusually quiet in those first minutes of the investigation. The device never went off. We sat and listened carefully to what was going on around us, however the room was still. Eventually, Ben wanted to try a new tactic to see if he could make things move along. He asked if anyone was comfortable being touched by an entity. As he asked, he pulled out a device that tests your heart rate. If you've been to the doctor's office, many nurses will test your vitals before seeing the doctor. This device was like that little monitor on your index finger to test your pulse. His hope was if a spirit perhaps touched someone's hand or shoulder, their pulse would quicken, and the device would record it, giving the group something to work with. The first step in communication.

I had many experiences in my investigations. The night before, I had the feeling of a hand around my throat. At the Mission Point Theater on Mackinac Island, I had the feeling of something tugging on my sleeve. It was not something I was uncomfortable with. I felt that these were the experiences we, as investigators, can use to learn more about the paranormal. I also felt it would be better for an investigator like me to do this rather than someone at the convention for the thrill who could potentially be traumatized by the experience, so when no one else spoke up, I volunteered. Ben placed the meter on my finger. We sat in complete silence after letting whatever spirit may have been with us know that it was okay to take my hand, touch my arm, or tug on my sleeve. After quite a while of sitting, it was obvious the test was going nowhere.

I did not feel anything of note other than exhaustion as the early morning hours were creeping upon us. I felt no touch, no feeling of anything being around me; it was still and quiet. My pulse remained the same the entire time it was on my finger. If there was an entity in that room, he or she was being shy. Not that I would blame the spirit. All these strangers poking around asking silly questions over and over. Ben placed it on his finger to make sure it was functioning, which the device was, so we put the experiment aside as another fail.

By this point, nothing had occurred to make us think there was an entity present in the room. We tried several things, including trying to get the spirit to push a water bottle off of the chalkboard, to no avail. By this time, people were getting either slap-happy or snippy as it neared the wee hours of the morning.

As we prepared to wrap up, Ben thought for a second and changed his mind about leaving. He decided to try one more approach before calling it a night. He stood up and pretended to be a stern teacher. He introduced himself as the new head of the class and explained that he needed to be respected. He started talking about paddling, a common form of punishment in many schools back in the day. Ben stated in a strict voice that if any children got out of line, the paddle could be used. After some time of playing a teacher, he took notice of a noise, a heavy and deep sigh. No one except Ben seemed to hear it. Suddenly it happened again.

"There, that, who did that?" I thought it may have been me, as I let out a little yawn, but he stated it wasn't a yawn, and it wasn't coming from where I was sitting. "It definitely wasn't a yawn. Who just went, *sigh*?" (He demonstrated the exact sound he heard.) Everyone insisted it wasn't them. No one made the breathy sound he was demonstrating. Ben seemed surprised when he saw our blank expressions. "You guys didn't hear that?"

Eventually, these noises became extremely common, and others started hearing the sounds. They were coming from above us, from behind us, from the hall, from right next to us. No one would take credit for these noises. After the first few times, everyone was sitting as still as possible, finally wide awake with no urge to yawn; yet the sighs were still happening. Being as quiet as we had become, it couldn't have been us.

There was a woman named Rosalyn Bown with our group who was also hearing the sighs. She joined Ben and took over asking a few questions. Rosalyn is a ghost hunter extraordinaire who was a member of the *Ghost Hunters* spin-off *Ghost Hunters Academy* on Syfy; she also appeared on the National Geographic Channel for paranormal programming. She is currently the co-founder of her own investigative group, "Perspective Paranormal Research."

"Do you need help? What kind of help do you need? Did someone do something bad to you?" Rosalyn asked with a voice of concern and compassion. After a few seconds there was a little creak, and then a very audible moan of exasperation, like someone trying to communicate and sighing with annoyance that no one seemed to understand. As soon as the voice was uttered, everyone stood up and looked around. It was one of the first times everyone heard the voice together as a group. Before this incident, some would hear it, some wouldn't. This time everyone was still, everyone was listening, and everyone seemed to hear it.

"What was THAT?" was all Ben could utter in shock.

"Check the hall please. I heard a little creak from over by the door," Rosalyn stated. One of the investigators ran to the door and looked out asking if anyone was out there. She returned looking confused.

"There's some water running in the bathroom, but…there's no one out there." Rosalyn took back the reins once people settled down.

"You need to know, we are here because we want to help you. Do you need help?" After Rosalyn finished asking, Tina Anderson sat up and looked at her K-II…

"Um, My K-II just started going off." The second she said that, there was a loud noise.

"What was that?" Ben asked, "That wasn't us?"

"Did it sound like it was over here?" I asked.

"Yeah, it was a…*sigh*…" I had heard it, but I thought I was hearing things. Apparently I was, but everyone else was hearing it as well. This was more than just a sigh; there was a male voice attached to it, it was more of a moan. It was something everyone heard, and everyone knew they were not the cause.

It was toward the end of the night, and the group with Ben still had to do the kindergarten room, however, only Rosalyn and I headed down. Once we reached the room, I set my equipment up while Rosalyn played back her recorder. Without needing headphones, you could hear the very sighs and moans that were occurring during our investigation with Ben. We looked at each other and knew instantly, Ben had to hear this. We ran back up to the second floor and played the audio for Ben. It confirmed what we were all hearing. It validated the shared experience.

At that, it seemed the night was over. In a sign of pure, exhausted slap-happiness, Ben treated us to very bad impression of Minnesotan and Yooper accents, a decent impression of John F. Kennedy, and a few cartoon voices. It seemed there was more giggling than paranormal investigation, so with that, the night came to an end. Everyone hugged new friends goodbye, and after a night's sleep at the hotel, I took the long drive home.

Upon arriving home to the great northern woods, I realized one of my pieces of equipment was missing—I could not find my recorder. After a frantic week without one of my recorders, Jenny Gurney's mother Bonnie amazingly found a recorder that went missing at the First Ward, and was able to get it back to me. In the heat of the moment when Rosalyn and I heard the sighs, we ran back to show Ben, and I left my recorder behind in the kindergarten room. While we were back where Ben was, Bonnie had found the recorder and mistook it for one of her's. After a hundred thank yous, the recorder arrived in the mail and was once again back in my hands. Once I had both of my recorders, it was time to upload the material and listen for anything unexplainable. I didn't have to wait too long.

I listened to the audio of the first night, fast-forwarding through the attic due to the noise and echoing. I came to when we had gone to the second floor bedroom with the beds from the Lemp Mansion. I heard myself claim one of the beds, I heard the sisters walk in, and I heard the giggles coming from the two sisters over the skeleton doll. After a few good chuckles there was silence. In the midst of the silence was this tiny little child's voice, a little girl, saying very clearly: "Hi Nancy…"

It was as clear as day. It was a child's voice. A child has a certain tone in their voice we lose as adults. Even women with higher voices still sound like adults with higher voices. This was a child. The voice was a little timid, like a shy little girl saying "Hi" to someone she just met.

I wish I had more closely eavesdropped on the sisters' conversations to see if they used their names when speaking to one another. Was one of them Nancy, and this little voice was trying to get their attention? One paranormal investigator I sent the EVPs to for a second set of ears suggested that to her, it sounded like "I'm Nancy" and not "Hi Nancy." Hi Nancy or I'm Nancy, maybe the sisters made the toy skeleton look like a lot of fun to play with, the little girl was trying to get their attention so she could play too.

A little later in the same room, Justin Chase Mullins, the psychic medium, was trying to get a feel for the beds. As he was concentrating, there was this soft voice. It was the same voice of that same little girl. She sounded bored and impatient, as she stated, "Come on and play!"

A few things struck me about these recordings. To me, the little girl sounded to be about five to eight years old. I place her at that age because, from baby to about four years old, boys and girls tend to sound alike. When they are about five, they start to sound like little boys and little girls, then by eight or nine years old, they start getting their big-kid voices, and then onto puberty where they start to grow into their adult voices and lose that childlike quality. This was definitely a child's voice, but obviously feminine, probably between five and eight years old. I knew for a fact there was no child between five and eight years old—in fact, there were no children present during the investigation— so it was odd.

Another thing that got me about the voice, whether she was saying "Hi Nancy" or "I'm Nancy," she was talking to the people in the room; yet no one responded to the voice. No one said, "Oh hey, hi," or "What's up?" There was no reaction to the voice, which could explain the impatience when I once again heard the girl whining, "Come on and play."

The other thing that struck me was that the voice was intelligent. The sisters were playing with a doll, and there is the sound of a little girl trying to introduce herself. Then the same little girl, impatiently asking for someone to play with her. If you look at the doll, and the fact the little girl wanted to play, it was obvious the spirit was speaking in direct relation to what was going on in the room.

In the kindergarten room after our group was done with the second-floor bedroom, I caught the sound of giggling, that coincided with the one time my K-II meter lit up and the Mel spiked; but I could not say for sure that the voice was from a spirit and not a natural person in the room, or passing by the room. Not much else happened in the way of audio.

The next room was the coal room. When we first got down to the coal room, we were all making small talk. "Oh Ben Hansen is going to be here tomorrow…" "It's already tomorrow"…"Has everyone taken Justin's tour?" "No" "No" "Yes" "No." "Okay…" as these small conversations were going on, there was an odd voice that sounded almost like, "All right, sit down."

The odd thing about the voice was that it sounded like it was right in the microphone of my recorders. What makes that odd is the fact that I was holding my recorders to my chest as I squeezed between people. You can hear my voice before this sound, but I sounded farther away—this was right into the mic. Someone would have had to speak into my chest, and I think I would have noticed that. This was unexplainable, especially since no one replied to the voice as if it went unnoticed.

After everyone sat down and one of the investigators explained about the "portal to hell" along the wall of the room, I relived that moment when I felt as if I was being choked. I could hear myself take in a deep breath, and let out a quivering breath. I did this a few times almost as if I was trying to catch my breath. I heard someone ask if I was okay, and I brushed it off like I was fine. I heard myself gag a little, then again try to catch my breath. I could picture myself at that moment saying a prayer in my head and making the sign of the cross on my knee. Once again someone asked if I was okay, and that's when I asked if there was a heaviness in the room.

After that, nothing seemed to happen. The couple who became frightened left the building, a few people decided to join another group in another room of the First Ward, and eventually Joe from *The Skeptical Edge* joined our now small group in the coal room. I heard the basketball roll out, and I heard myself explaining to Joe what had happened and then I heard Joe state:

"To the oppressive spirit here, what issue do you have with people?" There was a pause and then I started.

"You seemed to go for me when there was a guy in the room. Do you have issues with women?" In that pause between Joe and then myself speaking, there was this deep, almost mocking sounding laugh. To me it sounded like the stereotypical, mad scientist wringing his hands going "Muwahahaha." It was a bit shocking to hear.

I looked for other causes. It certainly wasn't any of us in the room; it was not the right frequency. It was quiet and echoed in an odd manner. There was no one else in the basement at the time; no one reacted to the sound so it wasn't heard. No machinery had kicked on, there was no construction work going on at the time outside, and the nearest factory closed at nine p.m., so it wasn't machinery. No matter what I used to debunk the sound, it still sounded like a male, mocking laugh, and it came after Joe asked what issue the spirit had with people; as if whatever spirit was there found what happened funny. I listened to it over and over, and it is definitely a laugh. I can't explain it in any other way.

The rest of the evening seemed quiet. I listened to the audio again to see if I missed anything. There were many other sounds that night that I put aside because, while not completely explainable, they were not clear enough to definitively say they were of paranormal origin.

After I had listened through the audio as much as possible and concluded I had taken all I could from it, I moved on to audio from the second night. That night I started and stayed in the coal room for most of the investigation. The moment the group I tagged along with that night entered the basement, we were greeted by a not-so-friendly voice. I heard our low voices as we quietly decided how we should divide up to cover the basement.

"Get OUT!" was heard very loud and clear in the microphone of the recorders I had just lightly placed down next to me. You could hear the other investigators and myself speaking, but our voices were much quieter and farther away from the recorders—our voices low whispers. The recorders were in my sight, so no one went near them at that moment. The voice was annoyed and above all else it went ignored. No one seemed to notice or react to what was just said.

Seconds later, those of us staying in the coal room started gathering our seats. I explained what happened the night before since they were not there when it happened. One gentleman asked me if there were any other men in the group. As I explained how the one man in my group couldn't handle what was happening, there was this noise, the only way I could describe it was a scream; it was muffled, it echoed in a weird way, no one seemed to notice the sound; it didn't fit what was going on with the group, so I could say it was not one of us. However, it seemed to be in direct response to things we were doing. Could it be the same spirit that uttered, "Get out" being fed up that we did not listen to his demand?

I turned the volume on my computer all the way up, cranked the volume on my audio program up by several notches, and then I turned the volume control on my headphones as high as it would go. The louder the sound, the more angry of a scream it sounded. It was as if whatever was there just took a deep breath and let out a wail as loud as he could.

I left the recorders in the room while I went into the hall for that time by myself. I regretted this decision considering it was in the hall where I saw that figure. Perhaps I could have captured an EVP while out there of whatever that figure was. It was a mistake I learned from; now I always have at least one recorder with me wherever I go, at all times. These are those little lessons you pick up on each investigation you perform.

When I returned to the coal room, one of the girls asked if whatever spirit was there wanted me to go back into the hall alone. As she asked, I heard the other investigator ask if she should offer herself instead. As this small conversation was going on, there was another voice, a voice that said, "Oh yeah" as if, "Yes send her back out here," or "Yeah I want you to go out instead." I wasn't overly impressed with the sound. It was very quiet and happened when others were speaking. I couldn't discount that the sound could have had a natural origin, so I set it aside.

There were a few other sounds from the coal room, but much like some of the sounds from the first night, I could not explain the sounds, but I couldn't deny that they could have had non-paranormal explanations. However, there was one as I left the coal room to speak with Keith Age that did give me pause.

As I exited the room, Keith was already discussing equipment and their various uses in investigations. I placed my recorders down quietly to avoid interrupting him. As he spoke, there was what sounded like a sigh of relief, and then a child's voice saying, "Okay, you're safe." I went back and listened to a few of the EVPs from the previous night; the "Nancy" and "Come on and play." It was the same little girl. It was unmistakable. It was the same voice, and the voice sounded relieved that we had exited the coal room. The sound was close to the microphone of my recorder, yet no one was standing near where I had placed the recorders except myself. And the only women in the basement besides myself, were sitting across from me, or standing up against the wall on the other side of me, farther away from the recorders. Whoever was relieved that no one was in the coal room now was not any of the investigators. Interestingly, it also came right at the time I started feeling the pressure lifting upon leaving the coal room.

Intrigued by this voice, I took the "Nancy" clip, the "Come on and play" clip, and this clip and spliced them together. I listened to all three on a loop; and there was no mistaking it—the voices were all the same. All three clips were high-pitched, childlike, female voices. They had the same tone, the same inflection, the same pitch. It was the same child.

Shortly after this incident, I headed upstairs with the group in the basement to investigate with Ben Hansen. Nothing of note happened during the early part of the investigation with Ben. I listened through the entire time we tried the little light device, then I listened as he placed the monitor on my finger. Just as nothing seemed to happen in person, nothing seemed to happen on audio. It wasn't until he began to pretend to be a stern teacher that things took a turn. Suddenly, there were unexplainable sighs coming from all over the room, some more dramatic than others.

The most compelling sound came after he started talking about the paddle. As soon as he mentioned the paddle, and if the children got out of line they would be paddled, I heard a heartbreaking sound. It sounded like a very young child crying, "No, No, NO, NOOO," as most children do when they are about to be punished for being naughty. The voice sounded younger than that of the little girl from the night before. It was such a sad and fearful cry. I was hoping I could find a way to debunk the sound, as I didn't want to believe this was the terrified child it sounded like.

I thought, what if it were some sort of animal and it only sounded like a child screaming "No no no?" I looked at the various animals that would be in a building. Being from the great northern woods, I was very accustomed to the sounds of various wildlife. I knew I could rule out bats. Bats do not sound like that at all. Much of their sounds are supersonic and would not display that loudly in the recordings. The wings of the bats flapping around would make more noise, yet there were no sounds of flapping of wings. This also ruled out pigeons. The owners stated there were no rodents in the building, and even if there had been, as someone who loves domestic rats and mice (they make amazingly wonderful pets for those who have the time to offer these sociable creatures), I know for a fact no mouse or rat has ever made a sound like that, even when cranky.

There were dogs in the building earlier in the day, a large breed Seeing Eye dog, a Chihuahua, and a Pomeranian. The large dog was automatically out. The owners of the Seeing Eye dog were not involved in the investigation. They had left after the day's festivities, as did the owners of the Pomeranian and the Chihuahua. None of the dogs were there at the time. Even if they had been, having worked in pet care, I know that even if in distress, there is no breed I can think of, especially none of the ones I met that day, that would make a sound like that.

My next thought was that perhaps it was a cat. Cats have been known to make many odd noises. So I contacted Heather Bram, one of the owners along with her fiancé Justin Libigs. She stated they had two little kittens locked in the one bedroom that wasn't open for investigation. That room was formerly the music room, which was (and still is) thoroughly soundproofed as to not interrupt other classes that were going on. Sound does not leak through that room. She has also never heard her kittens scream. They merely make tiny little mews that would not be audible from a soundproof room.

However, she stated that she would be more than happy to test the theory that sound could escape from the room, however unlikely it was. She asked in which room the EVP was captured in. I explained it was the second-floor room with the beds from the Lemp Mansion. As soon as she heard this, she immediately said it was impossible.

"There is simply no way those tiny kittens could muster up enough voice to escape a soundproof room, and be heard all the way into that room. There is no way. Even if they screamed, even if some sound leaked from the soundproof room, they'd never be heard in there." I asked if they were vocal, she stated they weren't. They mewed like kittens do, but they weren't screamers, or criers. Just playful talkers with small voices. In the end, I decided it could not have been the kittens, which were the only domestic animals there. And no wild animal, even if inside, could have made that sound. The sound was very human and, based on the volume and tone, had to be coming from within the room.

Still not wanting to call it a crying ghost child just yet, I turned to Jenny Gurney who had a lot of inside knowledge about the actual investigation.

"Do you know for a fact if there were any children there at the First Ward during the investigation? Maybe parents brought their child along, or maybe there were family/friends staying at the schoolhouse in one of the rooms closed to investigators that maybe had kids who woke up at that moment?"

"Definitely not," Jenny replied. "Children were not allowed in the schoolhouse during the investigation, so there shouldn't have been any kids there. It was clearly laid out by Justin that kids weren't allowed." The rule made sense because there were people walking all over until four o'clock in the morning, and we were dealing with the paranormal. Not an appropriate place for a child. "Why do you ask"? Jenny inquired. I explained the cry I heard. She told me that was very strange. "What is interesting about the room you were in; it's directly above the kindergarten room, and in the kindergarten room, there is a separate room where children were brought to be punished when they stepped out of line."

The punishment? According to Jenny—the paddle.

I eventually played the audio for Mr. Hansen who requested a copy that he could use for future lectures.

Did more than just the two children known to have died there, die in that building as Justin Chase Mullins saw when he read the building? Did those beds from the Lemp Mansion bring the spirits of souls who had died by some means in that mansion? Were dark forces brought to the First Ward because of bad things that happened there? Were the spirits in the residence buried at one of the nearby cemeteries just a mile up the way, who roamed until they found a place to stay in this schoolhouse? Perhaps these are souls in purgatory, attached to the building in death that they had an emotional attachment to in life.

Many questions remained except one. The one question I had answered was this; was the First Ward Schoolhouse in Wisconsin Rapids, Wisconsin, truly haunted? The answer I found there was yes. Yes, it most certainly was. I hope to one day return to find answers to the other questions I still have about those spirits. Judy, Heather, and Justin have quite a lot to contend with at the First Ward Schoolhouse—one of the more haunted places I have encountered.

Conclusion

There is so much we can learn from a paranormal investigation. That should be our main goal when we go to a location to investigate alleged hauntings—to learn more about the paranormal, to help those in need, to find answers to the unknown, and to further paranormal research. From these investigations, I learned quite a bit about the paranormal.

Spirits can travel. Much like we move from place to place, spirits (most of whom were people at one time like us) move from place to place. This was evident through spirits like Harvey. Harvey did not merely stay in the Straits Lodge or the theater of the Mission Point Resort, he moved between those places, between rooms, between floors. The same thing occurred with the spirits of the First Ward Schoolhouse. The little girl I heard in the second-floor room was the same one I heard in the basement. I found through speaking to other investigators like Jason and Grant from *Ghost Hunters*, that it was more than possible for a spirit to roam. Perhaps some of the spirits that reside in that building are buried in the two nearby cemeteries and found their way back. Spirits can move from place to place through attachments to places, objects, and people.

Spirits have emotions. At the private investigation, I left with the sense that the spirit who was there at the house felt compassion for the family and cared for the children. The spirit at the Paulding Lights had the ability to find humor in the situation at that moment going as far as to laugh at my brother and me. Many intelligent spirits have the same types of emotions they had when they were living people.

Spirits can physically manipulate objects. They can move balls, potentially turn on and off flashlights, and touch a person so that a person can actually feel the unseen hands on their body. They can turn on and off lights.

I learned that you should always own multiple digital recorders, and keep one on your person at all times because you never know what you may miss when investigating if you don't have one with you. Because I now know spirits can touch you or move objects, or roam from place to place, I've learned the importance of protecting yourself before and after an investigation and making sure you let spirits know they are not allowed to follow you when you leave.

All of these lessons tell me a little bit more about the paranormal, and give me an outline of new questions I can research. How can spirits physically manipulate objects when they have no physical form? How much energy does it take to move an object or turn on a light? When it comes to emotions they display, are these emotions genuine in the way we feel emotions, or are they remnants of their humanity; memories of emotions they re-create?

These are new questions I developed from the answers I found, which I can research in upcoming investigations. The more answers I find, the more questions pop up. Then finding the answers to those questions leads to more questions, discoveries, and research. And I will keep researching till no more questions remain. When that time comes, that will mean the paranormal has finally found a way to be proven to the world, including to skeptics, and it will become a science. That is what paranormal research is all about—helping people and finding answers until we know the unknown and learn to see what can't be seen.

Much like alchemists and physicians went on a quest to figure out what those spots inflicting so many people were back in the day of measles and small pox, and how to stop them, we continue our quest to learn, to discover the truth, and help people along the way.

Acknowledgments

Ben Hansen of *Fact or Faked*

Todd Clements, Author of *Haunts of Mackinac* for a lot of the Mission Point history

Kimberly Cenci

Justin Libigs

Jenny Gurney for the history of the First Ward

Heather Bram

Judy Carl

Justin Chase Mullins

To everyone who I have worked with on various investigations appearing in this book.

To Write the Author

If you wish to contact the author or would like more information about this book, please write to the author in care of Llewellyn Worldwide, and we will forward your request. Both the author and publisher appreciate hearing from you and learning of your enjoyment of this book and how it has helped you. Llewellyn Worldwide cannot guarantee that every letter written to the author can be answered, but all will be forwarded. Please write to:

Andrea Mesich
⁒ Llewellyn Worldwide
2143 Wooddale Drive
Woodbury, MN 55125-2989

Please enclose a self-addressed stamped envelope for reply, or $1.00 to cover costs. If outside the USA, enclose an international postal reply coupon.